Dear Mr Harper

Britain's First Green Parliamentarian

by

Robin Harper

with

Fred Bridgland

To Meg
with my very best wishes

Robin

BIRLINN

First published in 2011 by
Birlinn Limited
West Newington House
10 Newington Road
Edinburgh
EH9 1QS

www.birlinn.co.uk

ISBN: 978 1 84158 934 3

British Library Cataloguing-in-Publication Data
A catalogue record for this book is available from the British Library

Typeset by Iolaire Typesetting, Newtonmore
Printed and bound by MPG Books Ltd, Bodmin

To my dear wife Jenny, without whose encouragment and patience this book, and a lot else, would never have happened

Contents

Contents

List of Illustrations

List of Illustrations

Acknowledgements

My heartfelt thanks to Fred Bridgland, author and journalist, without whose professional guidance and assistance in rendering my words into readable English prose this book would quite definitely never have happened; to Elizabeth Garret, who provided Cliff Cottage, the lovely retreat on the cliffs near Stonehaven that gave Fred and me the space and time to get this written; and to my brothers, Euan and David, who gave invaluable assistance and information, and from whom I learned a lot that I didn't know about my own past.

Introduction

Shazam! The great Green Party breakthrough

At 4pm on Friday 7 May 1999, I was declared elected as Britain's first Green Party parliamentarian.

I was exhilarated beyond any telling or singing of it. It marked the end of a 12-year personal battle to achieve the Green Party's breakthrough into parliamentary politics and a chance to influence government thinking on the most daunting challenges of our times.

Commentators could not decide whether to take me seriously or treat me as some end-of-the-pier variety show performer. 'Now,' wrote Scotland's most distinguished political commentator,[1] 'the first-ever Green British member of parliament could hardly contain his bicycle clips. It was a strangely uplifting moment, like in American films when the unsophisticated good guy wins in the end. It will contribute enormously to the gaiety of the nation.'

I had stood in 11 previous elections – Westminster, European and local council – with the simple idea of getting the environment and other Green Party ideas on to the political agenda. Sometimes at school halls I hired for 'rallies' there was an audience of only two – the janitor and the janitor's dog. Throughout this time I had never actually expected to be elected: I simply saw my role as laying the foundations for some future Green Party success.

So, when it became clear that I had won enough votes to be elected, I was overpowered by feelings of elation. It was so wonderful that I was for a while in a complete haze.

The count had been a cliffhanger. In the early hours of the morning,

[1] Ian Macwhirter, political commentator for the BBC and the *Sunday Herald*.

six hours after polls closed the previous night, it was clear from the sizes of the piles of ballot papers on the tables at Edinburgh's Meadowbank Stadium that I stood a very good chance of becoming a Member of the Scottish Parliament (MSP). But the count teams were so exhausted that they were sent home to get some sleep before resuming in the afternoon. It looked as though I was running neck and neck in the Scottish second vote system[2] with Sir David Steel, who had led the Liberal Party in Westminster's House of Commons for 12 years. I was asked quite aggressively by television reporters how I would feel if I won at the expense of such a distinguished politician as Sir David. I said I would feel a twinge of regret if I beat him, but privately I also thought that if I lost I might mutter the words of Mo Udal, after he was defeated by the then obscure Jimmy Carter in the contest for the 1976 Democratic nomination for the Presidency of the United States: 'The people have spoken, goddamn them.' Udal, a Congressman for 30 years, was considered by many to be far too witty to be sent to the White House. He was also a devout Christian who ranked this among his favourite prayers: 'Lord, give us the wisdom to utter words that are gentle and tender, for tomorrow we may have to eat them.'

In fact, both Sir David and I made it to Parliament when the count resumed. He was subsequently elected the Scottish Parliament's first Presiding Officer, or Speaker.

By tradition, election acceptance speeches are kept short. You thank everyone from the returning officer to the police and finish by thanking your party and your family. I had a piece prepared acknowledging with some satisfaction that I had made history, just in case the press had not noticed! I felt in control of myself until I stepped up to the microphone and there was a huge cheer, not only from friends but from nearly all the supporters of other parties. I was close to tears as I repeated three times, 'I am the first Green . . .' before I got out the whole sentence: 'I am the first British Green to be elected to a parliament.' I said I hoped this would be as important a breakthrough

---

[2] Scotland's two-vote system, part constituency-based and part proportional representation, is explained later.

as Keir Hardie's election to Westminster in 1892 as the Labour Party's first-ever MP. I was still in a euphoric state when I was whisked away for media interview after interview, photograph after photograph. I managed to gather myself enough to outline my personal deepest belief – that Green would need to be the colour of the 21st century to secure the future of our planet.

We had already arranged a 'congratulations or commiserations' party at home. We could never have forecast the number of people who turned up on Saturday 8 May. Everybody came with something green, including a green plastic blow-up armchair; Greene King, a great-tasting beer loved by real ale enthusiasts across the world; Green Point champagne from Australia's Yarra Valley; a green tie or two, etc. Several hundred people must have passed through the house and the garden by the end of the day. My stepson Roy controlled the press interviews by monitoring my mobile for me. We took more than a hundred empty champagne and wine bottles to the recycling centre the next day.

Suddenly my life changed. Quickly I found I had become a national figure described as the 'shadow minister for absolutely everything', but at first I remained a bit of an anomaly. The environment was still seen by the majority of politicians and voters as just one minor issue among many others. During the first debate my fellow parliamentarians held on transport, climate change was mentioned only once – and that was by me!

I wondered how, as a one-man show, I would be able to make any difference about the kind of things I cared deeply about – such as overharvesting of fish stocks, deforestation, pollution of the environment and energy conservation in homes. And could I make such an impact that Green representation at the next election would soar? Now the real work was about to begin. It was a bit like jumping out of an aeroplane and wondering if the parachute would open.

There was also a wider responsibility beyond that to my Green Party colleagues and supporters. Scotland's Parliament had been re-established following a gap of three centuries after the country had lost its legislature and independence in 1707 under the Act of Union with England. A vibrant new political culture was being created, bringing policy decisions about key areas of Scottish life back home again, instead of being decided by a British Parliament hundreds of miles away at Westminster in central London in southern England. In an age of profound cynicism about politicians, I and the other 128 people elected to our infant restored institution faced a huge responsibility to make sure it worked in the interests of our countrymen. Re-establishing Scotland's Parliament was not a destination but a stop on a long ambitious journey that was only just beginning.

1

If you can teach in Glasgow, you can teach anywhere

It had all been a long journey from the time when, on graduating from Aberdeen University, I began my first job at a tough secondary school, Crookston Castle on the south side of Glasgow.

I had heard that Glasgow was so desperate for teachers, either certificated or non-certificated[1], that they were even recruiting from Canada. I was so eager to get out into the real world and do something practical with my life that I wrote to the Glasgow Education Department and was invited by return of post to attend an interview.

I found a clean shirt and tie and left at dawn for the 150-mile trip to Scotland's largest city. I was so poor at the time, in October 1962, that I had to hitchhike: my father had given me £15 to cover my graduation ceremony costs, but warned it was the last subsidy I would get from him. I began the journey from Aberdeen with a drunken truck driver who had not properly secured his load of empty fish boxes, which fell off at intervals along the route. I was mightily relieved that he could take me only as far as Stonehaven, 15 miles south of Aberdeen.

The interview in Glasgow was stunningly short. I was not even invited into a room. Somebody looked at me through a small window in a wall and asked if I had a degree and any experience. I said I had the degree and had run a youth club in Marylebone in London and been an instructor in the Sea Cadet Corps. He went away, came back with a sheet of paper with an address and phone number on it, and said: 'You can start at Crookston tomorrow.' The salary was £10 a

---

[1] A certificated teacher was one who had obtained a year-long postgraduate teaching qualification from a College of Education, often in conjunction with a university course in education history. I had yet to obtain my teaching certificate.

week. I managed to begin hitching back north before the light faded, packed my few things in Aberdeen in Pa's old green navy suitcase and just managed to catch the last train back to Glasgow the same evening. I was exhausted and must have arrived back in Glasgow towards midnight on a chilly late-autumn night. I had no idea where I was going to sleep.

As I set off from Queen Street station to find a cheap hotel, a small figure detached itself from the exit shadows and asked, 'Do you know where you're going, son?' I guess he was about 40 with the kind of taut pale skin and drawn face I came to think of as typical of Glasgow. I was 22 and so young-looking that if I shrank far enough down in my seat I would still have been automatically given a half fare by a bus conductor. I told the man I had no idea where I would sleep. He asked if I would like him to find me a hotel. For some reason I felt I could trust him. He led me along Bath Street, one of the long straight roads near the city centre, nipping down basements and up stairs until near the banks of the River Clyde he found me a boarding house, wished me luck and disappeared into the night. His was my introduction to that deep spirit of welcoming community that is the other face of Glasgow, so often portrayed as a mean city plagued by gang warfare and random violence. Later in life when I became resident in Edinburgh, Scotland's douce capital, 50 miles to the east of Glasgow, I realised people behaved differently on buses. You rarely see people speaking spontaneously to strangers on an Edinburgh bus: in those days, when I was new to Glasgow, you saw it all the time.

The next morning I took one of the city's orange, green and cream buses south across the river to Crookston Castle School, an ugly red building that has since been demolished. I entered the headmaster's study and stood at a respectful distance. He was a tiny man who glared at me over his spectacles. He did not invite me to sit and spat out just one question seven words long: 'Are you prepared to use the belt?'

I gulped in shock. He glared silently at me for a brief moment before barking: 'If you're not prepared to use it, you've not got a job.'

I reluctantly said yes because, although I was opposed to corporal punishment, I badly wanted the post. He reached in his drawer and handed me a brand new Lochgelly Number Three, a tan-coloured leather belt, or tawse, with two tails and so thick that it stood up straight. It had been designed in the 17th century by the Scottish education system to cause instant and ferocious pain to the palms and fingers of pupils judged to have misbehaved. I saw many of these wickedly effective instruments of torture. It became a thing of pride among some male teachers to boast that they had a really tough Lochgelly stained black with sweat from frequent use. At Crookston, they even belted girls.

I walked from the study with the tawse over my shoulder under my jacket, as was the custom, ready to administer fitting punishment within seconds of any misdeed or challenge to my authority.

My new colleagues told me I was filling the shoes of a dead man, a teacher who had a heart attack after getting over-excited watching Celtic Football Club score a goal at the east-end Parkhead Stadium. They were generally quite supportive, but the department heads had very little time for uncertificated teachers. Most of the kids in classes I was given were just waiting to leave school at 15 at the end of their third year of education, without sitting any public examinations. I was given sets of textbooks and just told to get on with it with the 'riff-raff' in the annexe, a collection of flat-roofed wooden huts across a four-lane road, with no bridge for the pupils to cross safely from the main school. One old hand among the senior teachers advised me: 'Just keep them quiet. And if you find you can teach in Glasgow, you'll be able to teach anywhere.'

The first thing that hit me in the annexe was the quite extraordinary smell of unwashed bodies of kids from deeply poor backgrounds who had been given the dreadful label of 'modifieds'. To be a 'modified' in Scotland was the equivalent of being ESN, or 'educationally sub-normal', in England and Wales – classified as a no-hoper in either system.

One of my first-year classes had about a dozen kids. The smallest, Bennett, just over four feet high, wore filthy trousers held up by string. His hair was cut almost to the bone, probably because of head lice. He had a perfectly round face and peculiarly round green eyes. He introduced himself by saying: 'It's nae fucking use trying to teach us.

3

We're modifieds.' He had a very low flashpoint and once threw a chair at me – it missed! The situation fired me up rather than making me cynical. I could hardly believe that educators could describe kids as 'modifieds'. I wanted then a better system that gave kids more respect, and that belief has stayed with me to this day.

Amazingly, I became very fond of Bennett and most of the troublesome children. Bennett was not a 'bad' person: he was just wired up and could not keep still. I realised that he had no hope of getting anything other than the most menial of jobs. I am sure he walked out into trouble. It is possible, I suppose, that he is dead by now. He was living in real poverty and Glasgow had, and continues to have, the lowest life expectancy of any city in the United Kingdom.[2]

My first truly big challenge came when I was told to fill in with a third-year English class until their regular teacher returned from sick leave. Naturally, they had fun testing my skills and ability to maintain discipline. One huge boy, Lachlan, had clearly been designated to test my patience and ability to keep control. I forget entirely now what it was he did. All I know is that it was so outrageous that normally he would have been sent to either the head of department or to the head teacher. Down the Crookston corridors I had heard the regular thwack of the belt being administered to children and I knew that if I reported him he would receive six of the hardest. It was a real dilemma. To do nothing or just give him some lines would have been a sign of incredible weakness that would have destroyed me.

So I called Lachlan out and prepared to give him two with all the might I could muster. His hands, as he crossed them over palms up, were the size of Belfast hams. He did not even flinch after the first stroke. He just smiled. After the second he turned to the class, said 'Aye, he can fair use the belt,' smiled yet again and sat down. I thought: 'Oh God, I really have lost it.' But I never had trouble from him or that class again – though the sobering thing was that I am pretty sure Lachlan was really running the class, not me.

I only used the belt three more times in a long teaching career, including one more time at Crookston.

---

[2] 'Life expectancy gap "widening"'. BBC News, 29 April 2005.

Later, when I taught at R.F. Mackenzie's revolutionary school at Braehead in Fife the only teacher who used the belt was a very nice and much-loved man, Bill Rintoul. He taught technical subjects and felt he had to use it occasionally for safety reasons. It was automatic that if anyone left their bench without permission it was three strokes of the belt. On one occasion when Bill saw someone moving and instinctively gave him three, the victim replied: 'Sir, I've been left two years. I've come in to see you and say thank you.'

Geography was the main subject I taught in the annexe. However, during my entire time at Crookston I was never visited by the head of geography. So I made up my own internal exams and taught what I could with the limited materials available.

I did do some teaching in the main school, where one of my favourite classes was a technical class, 2T, whose members were destined to take public examinations. They did some lovely work for me in geography and also played a spectacular practical joke in the summer of 1963. When the bell went for the end of a period a group of them gathered round my desk to ask a series of really good questions about the Great Navigators who first sailed around the earth. I was flattered by the interest they showed in my teaching skills and held forth learnedly to the torrent of questions. As quickly as they had gathered they also scattered. I felt pleased with myself, but then realised about one-third of the classroom chairs had disappeared. A guerrilla band had placed them on the roof while I was holding forth to the decoy group. I had little choice other than to laugh and climb up and remove the chairs myself. I actually found it quite funny and did not have the heart to be grumpy.

Another incident with that class was sad and taught me a salutary lesson that held for the rest of my teaching career: never, but never, threaten a punishment to a whole class if you do not intend to carry it out. It was a Friday afternoon and 2T were a bit restive. After a third or fourth time of warning them not to talk among themselves, I got unusually irritable, lost my rag and said, 'Look, we've got to get through this work by 3.30. The next person who speaks I'm going to belt.'

A deep silence descended before someone again spoke and, horror of horrors, it was Monahan, a sensitive, frightened wee boy who was so fragile that even the bullies left him alone. He looked like a frightened rabbit – disjointed, shambling and incredibly vulnerable. He was the last person I would ever have considered belting, but now I had to call him out to the front of the class to take the punishment I had threatened. I think the class was as shocked as I was. If they had taken a vote, I'm sure they would have said, 'Please, sir, don't hit him.'

I had trapped myself and he was already quaking before I prepared to hit him as gently as I could without looking weak. He immediately dissolved into uncontrollable tears after the first of two strokes, and I nearly burst into tears myself.

It was awful. It drove home to me that it was just plain wrong to hit people and that too many teachers in the education system were simply belt-happy. On the two occasions I used the belt in schools where I taught after Crookston it was, yet again, in order to protect the pupils from even worse punishments – severe beatings, being sent home or even expulsion.

What I experienced at Crookston showed me that the education system was not delivering properly for at least half the children trapped in it. It taught me more about what should not happen rather than what should, and I resolved that one day I would do things better. So, after a year at Crookston, I decided to return to Aberdeen and study at Aberdeen College of Education to obtain a Diploma of Education and become fully 'certificated'.

I smoked like a ship's funnel at the time. When my final day at Crookston arrived, I was delighted with the present I was given by Bennett and my other 'modifieds' – 60 carcinogenic Senior Service cigarettes and a box of Swan Vestas matches.

2

Turning Green

I remember precisely when I became a fully active Green. It was on 11 July 1985.

I was staying with friends in Germany, during a holiday from the school at which I was then teaching, Boroughmuir High in Edinburgh, when I saw on television a report about the sinking of the *Rainbow Warrior*, the flagship of the small fleet of boats belonging to Greenpeace, the global environment campaigning organisation.

I had become increasingly concerned about environmental issues while teaching modern studies at Boroughmuir and used every opportunity to include them in class discussions. In 1970 a book had been published called *Future Shock* by Alvin Toffler, an American sociologist and futurist, that I read some years later and which had an enormous impact on my thinking. Toffler argued that society was undergoing enormous structural change, a revolution from an industrial society to a 'super-industrial society'. He said this would overwhelm people, the accelerated rate of technological and social change leaving them disconnected and suffering from 'shattering stress and disorientation' – future shocked. His shortest definition of Future Shock was 'too much shock in too short a period of time.' He also popularised the term 'information overload'.

What particularly struck me, however, was Toffler's assertion that we would eventually begin to run out of natural resources, foreshadowing future books, articles and research papers describing ever more clearly the unsustainability of our economic system and the damage it was doing to the world's fragile environments.

I was also deeply influenced by Rachel Carson's *Silent Spring*, an epic work widely credited with helping to launch the environmental movement. Carson's book triggered widespread public concern about pesticides and environmental pollution. It documented detrimental effects of pesticides on the environment, particularly on birds. Carson said that DDT had been found to make thinner the egg shells of wild birds, particularly birds of prey, and result in reproductive problems and death. She also accused the chemical industry of spreading disinformation and public officials of accepting industry claims uncritically.

Silent Spring argued that uncontrolled and unexamined pesticide use was harming and even killing not only birds and other animals, but also humans. Its title was meant to evoke a spring season in which no bird songs could be heard – because they had all vanished as a result of pesticide abuse – and was inspired by a poem by John Keats, 'La Belle Dame sans Merci', which contains the lines 'The sedge is wither'd from the lake, And no birds sing.'

Carson, a distinguished writer on natural history even before the publication of *Silent Spring*, was violently assailed by threats of lawsuits and heaped with derision, including suggestions that this meticulous scientist was a 'hysterical woman' unqualified to write such a book. A huge counterattack against her assertions was organised and led by the whole American chemical industry, including Monsanto, Velsicol and American Cyanamid, duly supported by the United States Agriculture Department and the more supine elements of the media.

In response to the 1962 publication of *Silent Spring* and the uproar that ensued, President John F. Kennedy directed his Science Advisory Committee to investigate Carson's claims. Their investigation vindicated her work and led to an immediate strengthening of the regulation of chemical pesticides. DDT's use as a pesticide was finally banned in the U.S. in 1972.

However, despite having read *Future Shock* and *Silent Spring*, I did not see the environment as a political issue until the summer of 1985 when I holidayed with friends in the small German town of Friedrichshaven on Lake Constance, near the border with Switzerland. I had taught with Ann Kuypers during her classroom practice as a trainee teacher. She had a combined English and German honours degree from Edinburgh University and had met her Dutch husband-to-be, Bernd Kuypers, during her language study year in Munich. They had a common background. Ann's father had fought in the Norwegian resistance to German occupation in World War Two and Bernd's father in the Dutch resistance: they share four languages which they speak fluently between them. Ann and I both had a huge enthusiasm for the teaching of English, and the Kuypers have remained valued friends for more than 40 years.

And so, I was with them when the *Rainbow Warrior*'s sinking featured in a TV flash news report on 11 July 1985.

A Greenpeace photographer, Fernando Pereira, had died aboard the *Rainbow Warrior* when it sank the previous day in Auckland Harbour, New Zealand. The New Zealand government accused the 'action' branch of the French foreign intelligence service, the DGSE (*Direction Générale de la Sécurité Extérieure*), of attacking the vessel with two limpet mines to stop it leading a small flotilla of ships into French military zones around the Pacific Ocean's Moruroa Atoll to protest a planned Paris government nuclear test.

Two DGSE agents, Captain Dominique Prieur and Commander Alain Mafart – using Swiss passports and posing as a married couple, 'Sophie and Alain Turenge' – were arrested and jailed for ten years on a charge of manslaughter, reduced from one of murder. *Opération Satanique* was a total public relations disaster for France, and 20 years later the direct personal responsibility of the then French President, François Mitterand, was admitted by Paris.

Earlier that year an Edinburgh University lecturer, Tony Clayton, had thrust a leaflet about the tiny Ecology Party into my hand. I had put it carefully into my pocket and I now discovered it was still intact. I decided immediately to join the party, which then had about 5,000 members in Britain and which changed its name in 1987 to become the Green Party. I also joined Greenpeace, the international direct-action environmental campaign group, and Friends of the Earth, then Britain's most influential environmental campaigning organisation and now with almost one million supporters in more than 70 national organisations worldwide.

In September that same year, Clayton invited me to the annual general meeting of the Edinburgh branch of the Ecology Party. Although the branch had existed for some ten years it had only 35 members and had understandably made little or no impact. I asked Tony – now Professor of Environmental Science at the University of the West Indies in Jamaica – where the AGM was to be held. He had no venue and asked if it could be held at my flat. I agreed. There were five of us there, including Tony and me. The first item on the agenda was the election of a convenor and secretary: I was proposed and elected unopposed as both. I was glad of the chance and have not been out of office since! I suppose we bore at that time a faint resemblance to the Tooting Popular Front, the four-person would-be Marxist revolutionary party brilliantly created for a BBC comedy series with Robert Lindsay cast as the Afghan coat-wearing Wolfie Smith, the Che Guevara of suburban southwest London. Wolfie's revolutionary dream of lining his 'reactionary' enemies up against a wall for 'one last fag, then bop, bop, bop' was never remotely realised, not least because he got bogged down by life's everyday tedium: lack of money; his own reluctance to work, the misfortunes of his favourite football team, Fulham; and a girlfriend, Shirley, whose deeply conservative parents became his landlords and insisted on calling him Foxy, not Wolfie.

There was a health benefit for me from election to such high office: our 35 members stayed almost exclusively within running distance of my flat, and I was able to deliver party and Campaign for Nuclear Disarmament newsletters by hand while on my marathon training runs.

For the next four years I helped keep the party going and stood unsuccessfully in elections for Edinburgh Council, Westminster and, in 1989, for the European Parliament. I represented, at my own expense, our Scottish branch at party conferences in England and at several conferences of the Federation of European Green Parties.

The 1989 European Parliament election was a turning point in many ways. It was the best result that the Green Party had ever had in the United Kingdom nationally, winning more than two million votes

– 15 per cent of the overall turnout – and pushing the Liberal Democrats into fourth place. Nevertheless, under the first-past-the-post system under which European elections were then run we failed to gain any seats.

Despite winning so many votes, that year also marked a sad turning point for the English Green Party when it turned its back on its charismatic and most publicly recognisable leaders, Jonathon Porritt and Sarah Parkin, in a bitter and acrimonious internal wrangle. Everything had worked so well in the election campaign. They had led a superb TV party broadcast, still the best we have ever done. We had good candidates everywhere and sympathetic editorials appeared in some national newspapers. Environmental concerns were being reported to a far greater extent than ever before. Everything was on our side, but it was all blown when Porritt and Parkin lost patience and resigned, feeling they had failed to convert the party into something electable because of what Paul Vallely, *The Independent*'s environment correspondent, described as 'all the wild, woolly, bright greens in it who wouldn't compromise their purist "no leaders here" idealism.' Vallely said Porritt and Parkin became frustrated with the tendency of the party to level down all talent rather than strive to become electorally effective. Porritt particularly made enemies when he said unequivocally that collective leadership would not work, and indeed it was only after the Green Party in England came to the same conclusion many years later that it managed in 2010 to get its first representative into Westminster.[1]

In Scotland, I had had to work out a way of hitting every part of the electorate in that 1989 election with a small core of four helpers and 20 party activists in Edinburgh. Our tiny press office measured six feet by six feet, just enough room for a couple of chairs, a desk, a cupboard and a photocopier. We leafleted the whole of Scotland on election Freepost. The logistics of Freepost are huge. The leaflets have to be exactly the right size to meet Post Office regulations. They can only be

---

[1] *Jonathon Porritt: A subtle transition from green to shades of grey*, by Paul Vallely. *The Independent*, 31 August 2002.

used to put your own point of view and may not contain derogatory material about opponents. They have to be counted into 50s by the party and sent out batched accurately for each postal district. It is living proof that in our democracy you can be guaranteed to get your message through the nation's letterboxes with practically no cost other than huge amounts of physical and organisational effort. By election day I was so exhausted that I could not even drive. In Scotland the result was 10 per cent of the total vote in Scotland. The 15 per cent vote share for the UK as a whole would have meant, in almost any other European country, that we would have won seats in the European Parliament for the first time.

Our little band of brothers and sisters knew we still faced a long haul before we could have any real influence on political decisions, especially under the 'first-past-the-post' or 'winner-takes-all' Westminster constituency system which has no room for many substantial minority voices. This voting system is not only disproportional, it is arguably undemocratic. For example, in a constituency with three fairly evenly matched candidates, the winner can win and take all with only 34 per cent of the votes. In a competition with 10 contestants, a winner could gain 100 per cent of the representation with only 11 per cent of the vote: This can happen even if the majority of voters intensely dislike the winning candidate.

The effect in Scotland of the encouraging 1989 vote was immediate and spectacular. Our membership tripled after the election, and we established a separate Scottish Green Party in an amicable separation from the Green Party of England and Wales, with which we continued to maintain close relations. There existed then at least half a dozen active remnant left-wing parties in Scotland who were still vaguely organised but rarely if ever bothered to contest elections. The bulk of our new membership almost certainly came from these parties and others who simply saw us as challenging the whole system of British politics. We were also joined by many people who were environmental campaigners but did not realise that we had a very well-developed set of left-of-centre social and economic policies. The party's post-election euphoria was reasonably controlled: we avoided an ambitious spending spree or over-organising centrally.

But it was depressing to observe our membership fall steadily again once the initial rapture evaporated.

At every step in the history of the Green Party since I joined we have had discussions about how to position ourselves on the political spectrum and how we want to be seen by the average voter. With certain exceptions, we have until fairly recently been consistently misrepresented by the press. I remember, for example, attending an English Green Party conference in 1990 dressed in a pin-stripe suit and tie. There was considerable press interest following the European election success, but photographers concentrated almost entirely on those few of our members who sported open-toed sandals, beards, long hair and exotic brightly coloured garments. We had yet to be taken really seriously.

It was at this time that I became involved in a campaign for a Scottish Assembly. Hopes for a devolved parliament had been ditched in a controversial 1978 referendum held under James Callaghan's UK Labour government, defeated in a general election in the following year by Margaret Thatcher and the Conservative Party. We thought a Labour Party led by Neil Kinnock might deliver devolution if it won the 1992 Westminster election. But Kinnock took Labour to defeat, blaming newspaper criticism rather than his own prematurely triumphal speech-making that repelled large numbers of voters.

That year I was invited to Helsinki to represent the Scottish Green Party at the conference of the Federation of European Green Parties. Despite the fact that we did not yet have devolved government I was permitted to argue for Scotland to be represented separately from the rest of the UK at the conference. The French and Spanish Greens were very much against, mainly because they foresaw problems with Catalonia and the Basque Country, where significant numbers wanted independence or substantial devolution. However, there were many delegates from smaller previously Soviet-controlled states from behind the former Iron Curtain, which had just fallen, who were very keen to support another small state to balance the huge influence of the French, the Italian and principally the German and Austrian Green parties. I won the right to speak as a Scottish Green by just two votes, but the real reward followed within a decade with the creation of a Scottish Parliament.

One consistent vow in the Scottish Green Party was to fight for electoral reform, which we thought would happen one day, and keep stating our Green convictions. By 1992 the Scottish Green Party's headquarters again amounted to a photocopier in my house. We had hardly any money and people were quarrelling about many totally irrelevant matters. At a poorly attended AGM that year, with only about 30 people present, I was involved afterwards in a discussion about whether to wind up the Scottish party as a separate entity and rejoin the England and Wales party. Close to furious, I strenuously resisted the proposition, won the case and with the help of a man named Gavin Corbett, easily the hardest-working member the party has ever had, reorganised and downsized our organisation and kept it going for the next seven years, awaiting an opportunity to transform our fortunes.

In September 1994 I managed to combine getting married, to Jenny Carter, with being a Green Party candidate in that year's European Parliament election. I lost and only just failed to get my cash deposit back, which in terms of Green Party politics counted then as a success.

I kept going with the faith of some kind of religious fanatic, not knowing then that with the creation of a Scottish Parliament in 1999 would come a second vote system with some members elected by proportional representation. I simply hoped that I would live long enough to see a Briton elected somehow as a Green Party representative to a parliament in Brussels, London or Edinburgh.

In the 1997 British general election campaign the ruling Labour Party promised to create a devolved Scottish Parliament if a majority of Scots voted for it in a referendum, and it kept its promise. More than 74 per cent of the electorate voted 'yes' in the referendum on 11 September 1997. The creation of a Scottish Parliament saw a revolution in British electoral law. While 73 of the 129 members of the new Parliament would be elected from constituencies in the traditional first-past-the-post way, it was agreed that the remaining 56 would be elected by proportional representation to allow a handful of minority voices to be heard officially in the country's top democratic forum.

The scale of the proportional representation share of the vote, from regional lists, fell far short of our wishes. But here at last was our chance to play a real part in national politics. We began preparing for the 1999 election campaign.

3

Orkney days amid warfare

I was born on 4 August 1940. Looking through my father's effects after he died in 2002, I discovered one of those tiny little diaries that can fit into a top pocket. It was slim and bound in soft brown leather with 1939 stamped in gold. I opened the diary with some trepidation. It was almost entirely empty, with 4 November 1939 among the exceptions. The entry for that day reads: 'My birthday. Took a day's leave. Robin probably started.'

Pa and my mother were living on the Orkney Islands. At the onset of the Second World War, Pa was serving on HMS *Iron Duke*, a venerable old battleship being used as a training vessel but which had been the flagship of Admiral Sir John Jellicoe at the 1916 Battle of Jutland, the greatest naval battle of the First World War.

Within hours of Britain declaring war on Germany in 1939, *Iron Duke* was sent north from Portsmouth to Scapa Flow, in the Orkney Islands, to do service as an administrative base, depot ship and anti-aircraft platform. Accompanying *Iron Duke* was the rest of the British Reserve Fleet – a few battleships and cruisers and scores of other ships left over from the First World War – to protect the Scapa Flow-based Home Fleet, the navy's main battle force in European waters. On board *Iron Duke* was Sir Wilfred French, appointed Admiral commanding Orkneys and Shetlands, with Pa, by then a lieutenant-commander, as Assistant Secretary. Mum and Pa had only recently got married in London at Chelsea Register Office and she followed him north from Portsmouth to lodge with a Church of Scotland Minister and his wife in the manse at Longhope on the Island of Hoy where Admiral French had his headquarters aboard *Iron Duke* moored at the village of Lyness.

Scapa Flow, on whose shores I lived in my early years, is a body of water some 120 square miles in area and surrounded by a ring of islands sheltering it from Atlantic Ocean and North Sea storms, effectively creating one of the world's greatest natural harbours. It has been used by vessels for thousands of years. The Flow should have been a secure anchorage for the British fleet, but just six weeks into the war, on 14 October 1939, a German submarine, U-47, commanded brilliantly by Lieutenant Günter Prien, navigated its narrow channels, sunken blockships and racing tides to get into the harbour's heart. There he found the battleship HMS *Royal Oak* and fired a salvo of three torpedoes which blew a hole in her armour. A fireball raced through the ship: she rolled onto her side and sank after 13 minutes. There was heavy loss of life: 833 of *Royal Oak*'s 1,234 men were killed that night or died later of their wounds. On calm days, the upturned hull of *Royal Oak* – now an official war grave, with the remains of many of the dead sealed within her – can be clearly seen beneath the surface of Scapa Flow.

Three days after *Royal Oak*'s sinking, Pa and the crew of *Iron Duke* on the other side of the Flow were calmly going about their duties through yet another warning by sirens of German 'air raids'. These were usually forays by reconnaissance aircraft, but on this occasion an enormous explosion lifted *Iron Duke*'s stern out of the water. Pa rushed from his office, two decks below the top deck, and had just reached Admiral French's living quarters above when another explosion caused the ship to list heavily to port. One bomb had plunged down *Iron Duke*'s aft (or rear, if you are a landlubber) funnel, exploding in the boiler room, which flooded together with two ammunition magazines. Pa was thrown to the deck and, on staggering to his feet, found Admiral Jellicoe's coat draped over his shoulders: it had been in a glass exhibit case in Admiral French's quarters. Reaching the top deck he saw a plume of smoke on land where one of four attacking Luftwaffe Junkers Ju-88 bombers had been shot down, and a descending parachute. The German airman was found dead and badly burned and was buried in Lyness Cemetery under a 'Negative' flag – black crosses on a white background. The dead pilot's aircraft was the first of the war to be destroyed over Britain by an anti-aircraft gun – but the Junkers had also dropped the first German bombs of the war to land on British territory. *Iron Duke* was towed into Gutter Sound and beached in shallow water, while Pa and the rest of the Admiral's staff established new offices ashore in Lyness. *Iron Duke* remained in use as a platform for anti-aircraft guns: she was sold as scrap at the end of the war and broken up in Glasgow.

Shortly before she was attacked *Iron Duke* had been visited, on 16 September, by Winston Churchill, who was then First Lord of the Admiralty but became Prime Minister the following year. Churchill stood on a grating on the quarterdeck and, addressing ships' companies from around the Flow, said he had stood on the same spot aboard *Iron Duke* in the same capacity, as First Lord of the Admiralty, precisely a quarter century earlier at the beginning of the First World War.

Following the successful German hits, Churchill – who with typical magnanimity described Lieutenant Prien's attack on *Royal Oak* as 'a remarkable exploit of professional skill and daring' – ordered the construction of a series of causeways to block the eastern approaches to Scapa Flow. Designed to prevent any possible repeat of Prien's valiant feat, and supporting an inter-island road to this day, they were built by Italian prisoners of war held on Orkney and are known as 'Churchill barriers'.

Barely a week before *Royal Oak*'s catastrophic sinking and the follow-up bombing of *Iron Duke*, King George the Sixth stood on the top deck of the latter to address Scapa Flow crews. Among the men, in a fisherman's heavy jersey, was 52-year-old Joseph Watt who had won the Victoria Cross for gallantry during the First World War while serving as the captain of a drifter fishing boat, armed only with a six-pounder gun, on patrol duties in the Adriatic Sea. One day he engaged a heavily armed Austro-Hungarian cruiser, forcing it back to its home port despite facing overwhelmingly heavy firepower. The King, passing along the ranks, noticed the medal pinned to Skipper Watt's chest and asked in his habitual stutter: 'Wh-wh-where d-d-did you g-get the VC?' Back in a broad northeast Scotland accent came the serious reply: 'Buckingham Palace, sirr' – an answer that somewhat nonplussed His Majesty.

*   *   *

Mum was not happy lodging at the church manse and was delighted when she and Pa were able to rent a tiny stone cottage on Hoy, one of Orkney's 20 inhabited islands – another 50 are uninhabited. Orgill Cottage directly overlooked the Flow. It had two small rooms, a kitchen with an old-fashioned stove and an outside bucket lavatory. We got water from a stream that flowed past the back of the cottage from Ward Hill, which rose above our home. The ashes of both my parents have been scattered in this stream. Our main furniture consisted of an iron bedstead, a wooden table covered in ancient oilcloth, one wooden chair, a small armchair and a framed paper portrait of Queen Victoria. The bed mattress was sodden when Mum and Pa moved in and had to be dried out for weeks in front of a peat fire. Despite Orgill Cottage's spartan condition, my parents looked back on the years they spent there as among their happiest.

It was in Orgill Cottage that I was conceived. Mum was unwell in the final stages of her pregnancy in the summer of 1940, so the base doctor ordered her to be transferred to the mainland and the maternity hospital in Thurso. To ensure getting her there before I arrived, she was put aboard a fishing drifter that carried the post between Lyness and Scrabster, a small harbour on Thurso Bay, from where she was taken by taxi to the hospital. As Pa was on duty he was unable to be at my birth: with Britain under assault, the Royal Navy did not make exceptions for that kind of thing, not least because Scapa Flow had become World War Two's first target of major German attacks by sea and by air.

Adolf Hitler's intent, as my obscure birth was taking place in Britain's far north, was to soften up our islands in preparation for a German military invasion. As I made my first cries Winston Churchill and Air Chief Marshal Hugh Dowding were preparing for an epic fight. The Battle of Britain began four days after I was born in a clash involving 150 aircraft over the south coast of England in which the Royal Air Force lost 19 planes and the Luftwaffe 31. On the eleventh day of my life the Luftwaffe launched 1,790 sorties against Britain, downing 34 RAF warplanes for 75 losses of its own.

It is a truism that in the month of my arrival my destiny lay in the hands of Dowding and Churchill who, when I was just two weeks old, made his famous speech praising the RAF's Battle of Britain pilots:

19

Never in the field of human conflict was so much owed by so many to so few. All hearts go out to the fighter pilots, whose brilliant actions we see with our own eyes day after day . . . The gratitude of every home in our island, in our Empire, and indeed throughout the world except in the abodes of the guilty goes out to the British airmen who, undaunted by odds, unweakened by their constant challenge and mortal danger, are turning the tide of world war by their prowess and their devotion.

That month, Churchill and Dowding estimated that the RAF and Britain were within 24 hours of defeat if the Luftwaffe managed to strike the ultimate killer blow. Tumultuous though the times were, however, my first years of life seemed untroubled on the Orkney Islands by the huge war for the world going on elsewhere, over England's and Scotland's skies and right across Europe, North Africa and the Far East. A few months after I was born the Home Fleet's flagship, the battlecruiser *Hood*, sailed out of Scapa Flow with other ships to intercept the German Navy's biggest ship, the battleship *Bismarck*, and the cruiser *Prinz Eugen*, as they broke out into the Atlantic to catch and destroy convoys in transit between North America and Britain. *Hood*, the flagship of Rear Admiral Lancelot Holland, and other fighting ships encountered the German vessels west of Iceland on 24 May 1941. *Hood* was hit by shells first from *Prinz Eugen* and then the *Bismarck*. A huge jet of flame shot upwards from *Hood* followed by a rumbling explosion. She split in two and within three minutes had slid to the bottom of the Atlantic with the loss of 1,415 of her 1,418 crew, including Admiral Holland.

Churchill responded by issuing a famous order: 'Sink the *Bismarck*.' It spurred a relentless pursuit by the Royal Navy, and the pride of the German fleet was intercepted and sunk off the southwest coast of Ireland on 27 May: 1,995 of the *Bismarck*'s crew of 2,200 died.

* * *

My earliest memories of the Orkney Islands are of Hoy's windswept moors, the huge vault of the sky and the extraordinarily clear, crystalline colours of the sea in Scapa Flow. You could see deep down into the water – gorgeous emerald greens, shading off into deeper greens and blues and purples. Wind was omnipresent. There was constant movement of sky and sea and of grasses and heathers shaking in the wind. There were very few trees. There was lots of water in deep peaty streams and ditches. The sunrises and sunsets were amazingly beautiful, but the winters were incredibly long and dark and punctuated by 78rpm records playing on my parents' wind-up gramophone, which I still have. Everything smelled of the sea, and there was always the sound of the wind and the mewing of seagulls, a 'beginning of time' experience, almost primeval. You could not avoid being part of the natural environment. Orgill Cottage was hunched against the elements, and they assaulted you the moment you stepped out of the door.

We later moved into a Nissen hut – a prefabricated structure made from a half-cylindrical skin of corrugated steel and used widely by Britain and the United States on their military bases – near Lyness, a larger home where we were joined by my Aunties Dorea and Edie-Kay, Pa's sisters. Mum was also given some domestic help from the Navy in the shape of a stoker, 'Organ' Morgan, who every morning lit the old-fashioned cast-iron range, a great big black monster, that heated our hut and on which Mum did all the cooking. 'Organ' Morgan was a wonderfully kind man who made me a train set from scraps of wood. He painted them bright blue, silver, green and red and I played endlessly with them. I have one of the carriages to this day. Although I did not realise it at the time, my folks were desperately poor because they had lost all their possessions when a German bomb destroyed the warehouse where they were stored in Portsmouth.

The Orcadian part of me that remains is that I can be very happy completely alone on top of a very windy hill. Bad weather does not distress me. I love wind and rain. I believe it was in those early Orkney years that environmental awareness was imprinted on me. Or, perhaps, I was born with 'Green genes?' In summer we roamed with great abandon, although one adventure might have ended my careers before they were even dreamed about. My little brother Euan and I found a wooden box washed up on a tiny sandy beach at the bottom of a cliff, and we decided to sail in it to sea. Several yards out we began sinking.

Water was pouring through knotholes. We swam frantically for shore in ice-cold water and only just made it.

I began my schooling in Orkney, but recollect only a very cold and drafty schoolroom with a squeaky slate blackboard and half a dozen little wooden desks where we wrote with chalk on individual slates but where I quickly learned to read, becoming a voracious bookworm for the rest of my life.

On my fifth birthday, just after the war in Europe had ended, I was promised a cake aboard one of the Navy's corvettes. It was wonderful. The vessel was decked in colourful bunting and ceremonial guns boomed out. Pa, Mum, Euan and I were piped aboard from a ceremonial barge. The crew sang Happy Birthday and a Marine band played the national anthem. All for me. Or so I thought until my mother gently explained to me, downstairs in the mess, that the singers and the band were celebrating the birthday of Queen Elizabeth, wife of our then monarch, King George the Sixth. She had been born on the same day as me, but a mere 40 years earlier!

*　　*　　*

Admiral Wilfred French was forced to retire from active service following the sinking of *Royal Oak* and was replaced by Admiral Patrick Macnamara, with Pa promoted to be his Secretary. Macnamara, an enormous man with a flaming Irish temper, had been recalled from retirement to replace the unfortunate French. Macnamara's own glittering career seemed also to have come to an unfortunate end in 1936 when, as a Captain commanding the battleship HMS *Nelson*, his vessel became stuck on a mudbank at the mouth of Portsmouth Harbour with the then new commander of Britain's Home Fleet, Admiral Sir William Henry Dudley Boyle, aboard. Seven destroyers were summoned to create great waves in an effort to sweep mud away with their wash: this wheeze succeeded only in wrecking a pontoon bridge a mile away. Finally, the *Nelson* floated off after Macnamara emptied oil tanks and ammunition magazines on to a flotilla of loading barges.

Macnamara was sent into early retirement with the rank of rear-admiral. The mud onto which he nosed the *Nelson* happened to be named the Hamilton Bank, prompting the captain of Portsmouth Dockyard to send the following signal: 'It is good to see a Nelson mounting a Hamilton again!' – a reference, clearly, to the adulterous affair between Admiral Lord Horatio Nelson and Emma, Lady Hamilton, the young wife of the British ambassador to Naples, the greatest scandal of the age two centuries ago when Emma gave birth to Nelson's daughter Horatia.

My Orkney Days ended at the age of six when my father was transferred first to London and then Ceylon, now Sri Lanka, and I was sent to a dreadful boarding school at the other end of Britain.

4

Campaigning for Scotland's new Parliament

The creation in 1999 of a new Scottish Parliament, after a gap of 300 years, offered the Green Party an unprecedented chance to make a political breakthrough – because, unlike the Westminster Parliament system, a limited number of members were to be elected by proportional representation (PR).

The framers of the new assembly's constitution included representatives of the Christian churches, industry, voluntary organisations and other branches of civil society, as well as political parties. Most felt that partial PR would be more democratic than Westminster's wholly first-past-the-post constituency system.

The consequence was that Scotland adopted a one-person, two-vote system, with the first vote going on a purple-coloured ballot paper to candidates in a straightforward constituency system, *à la* Westminster, and the second going to party candidates, on a peach-coloured ballot paper, in a rather complex PR procedure.

We decided not to use the party's limited funds in campaigning for the first vote since we knew that system was stacked against us. Instead, we put all our efforts and limited funds into the second vote campaign, explaining the system to electors and what it would mean if they used their second vote tactically. We knew there were huge numbers of environmentally committed or aware people out there who felt a Green Party vote was wasted in the Westminster system but who could be persuaded to vote Green in a PR system if they became convinced that a Green could actually make it into the legislature. One estimate was that half a million Scots were members of environmental organisations, and they might want to give their second vote to us.

There were already several kinds of PR system in use in other democracies in Europe. The most popular was the 'additional member system' that we, the British, had invented and imposed on defeated Germany at the end of the Second World War. It was the most democratic and accountable system that we could think of at the time to protect Germans against the possibility of Nazis or Stalinists ever seizing power again. Since Germany had used the system for nearly 60 years, creating one of the fairest and most vigorous democracies in Europe, we decided that if it was good enough for post-Second World War Germany it would be good enough for Scotland and a restored Scottish Parliament.

We urged people to use their second vote to shake the cosy complacency of the mainstream parties and confound the political mammoths. In addition to our voter 'education' crusade, we decided we also needed a really good unconventional 'song and dance' propaganda drive. We needed to work the system.

My own 'Dr Who' rainbow-coloured scarf and black fedora became campaign icons. I had bought my first rainbow scarf in the 1970s from Studio One in St Stephen Street, Edinburgh's equivalent of London's Carnaby Street. Some people in the party were a little embarrassed by the scarf and hat. They protested that the image they projected was 'too Green', too iconoclastic and too juvenile. They were keen, as I was also, to shake off the 'hippie' image given us by the press: they wanted to adopt a more businesslike profile, a more grey and 'professional' appearance, with me and other leaders wearing smart conventional suits and sober-coloured ties. I resisted because my scarf, hat and tie foible gave the party instant public recognition. Indeed, people quickly began to complain to me if I turned up at events without them: they liked what was actually more than a personal gimmick. The scarf, hat and ties had become part of me down the years. I'd been collecting bright and flowery ties since the early 1960s. I had so many that when they were all laid out at the last school I taught at they went up and down the assembly hall six times – a distance of 400 feet: I auctioned some to raise money for the party.

We adopted the slogan 'Vote Green 2', a play on the fact that, whatever people's choice of first candidate, they could vote Green *too*!

We worked hard to persuade Scots that a PR vote for us would not be wasted, hammering home the message that a Green cross on the second ballot paper really could get the Green Party into Parliament.

My wife Jenny put me in touch with a designer, Martin Budd, who, in exchange for a bottle of wine, carved a five feet-high, one foot-wide polystyrene '2'. I gave it an undercoat of fluorescent yellow, to give it a bit of bounce, before applying a top coat of fluorescent green. It was a huge success. I took the '2' with me everywhere for three weeks in outdoor campaigning. I once took it upstairs on a bus and stuck it on the front seat where everybody could see it. The bus management got stuffy, rang the driver and ordered him to tell me to 'tak' it doon.' I moved the '2' onto a side seat where it was still visible anyway. I also had the idea of flying it behind a kite on Bruntsfield Links, an open area in southern Edinburgh, for a press photo opportunity. I bought the biggest kite I could find, but sadly it was unable to lift the '2' into the air. Happily, however, somebody turned up on a bicycle with a trailer and we trundled our bright green '2' around for the whole of the campaign. The National Museum of Scotland liked the '2' so much that its curators asked if they could have it as part of their historic election record. And so instead of being dumped in a garage, it now lives in storage in the National Museum. One day I hope it will be taken from storage for public display.

I concentrated my campaign effort on Princes Street, the Scottish capital's famous thoroughfare running beneath the castle perched on its towering volcanic rock. The possibility of a Green breakthrough energised our supporters. After 14 years of unrewarded endeavour, people now came out and worked with extraordinary enthusiasm. Volunteer 'Earth Warriors' arrived from Yorkshire, Germany, Austria and all over to support the campaign. Our offices were awash with a variety of volunteers of all ages, some of them not party members.

The PR vote was divided between eight designated constituencies. I was the number one Green PR candidate on the list in the Lothians constituency, with Edinburgh at its heart. It was impossible to meet all 750,000 people entitled to vote in the Lothians, but I obtained figures that showed 75,000 people walked along Princes Street every day. So we put Green Party tables at each end of the street and handed out our pamphlets and business cards which said Vote Green on one side and gave our ten key campaign promises on the other. That way we knew we would reach far more people than by trying to knock on every door in the constituency. Although we knew that personal door-stepping is by far the most effective way of campaigning, we simply did not have the numbers to be able to do this properly. I was often joined while campaigning by my teenage stepson Roy and his friend Andrew Doig, who became my loyal assistants in subsequent elections.

As the campaign went on I gained enough confidence to consider putting a bet on my becoming a Member of the Scottish Parliament (MSP). I reckoned my winnings might cover some of the money I'd spent in contesting eleven previous lost elections. I went into one of the bigger betting shops and asked for odds, but the bookies refused to accept my wager. One said: 'You must know something we don't know!'

Long ago, in my personal life, I had decided that persuasion was better than confrontation. I applied that part of my philosophy to my politics, which were a serious matter for me but also fun. I believe in positive campaigning and always counselled the party that we have such an important positive message to give that we would simply waste valuable time and space if we engaged in the kind of knocking, yah-boo politics that too often characterises the conduct of the other political parties and which lowers the tone of debate. Being courteous to even the most ferocious of critics paid off to the extent that one newspaper columnist wrote: 'Can Robin Harper really be a politician? He must be one of the least likely politicians in the history of democracy . . . He does not look like a politician because he smiles with his eyes, listens, shows infectious enthusiasm over the smallest thing and does not claim to know all the answers.'[1] Of course, I liked that!

We hoped that the Scottish Parliament would elect by PR some unsullied political virgins who, instead of the usual suspects, the professional politicians, would bring vitality, fresh ideas and innovative talent to the new institution – entrepreneurs, artists, farmers,

[1] Anna Burnside, the *Sunday Herald*, 25 April 1999.

27

writers, peace campaigners, community workers, foresters, the odd poet or two, committed rebels and veteran educators and political mavericks such as me.

We fielded 41 candidates across the eight regional list constituencies. On our most wildly optimistic days, we hoped that eight Green Party members would be elected to the Parliament from the 56 who would be elected on the PR 'additional member' system, with seven of these MSPs being elected from each of eight regional list constituencies across Scotland.

We did not achieve our wildest dreams. I was the only Green to be elected to that first Scottish Parliament, with nearly 23,000 votes, seven per cent of the total second ballot in the Lothians. In other constituencies some Green candidates had won more than 10,000 second votes, not enough to get themselves elected but enough to encourage me to think that if I worked hard and effectively enough we could increase our representation by the time the second Scottish Parliament election would be held in 2003.

5

Mum, Pa and other relatives

Both my parents' families were exotic and turbulent in different ways. Pa's parents were business people in pre-Communist China and Mum came from Gillingham, a town on the River Medway in the southeast England county of Kent. Cheek by jowl with Gillingham was the Royal Naval Dockyard at Chatham, which for two centuries was key to the Navy's long period of supremacy at sea. But the dockyard was closed in 1984, after a short reprieve for the Falklands War, leading to the demise of the local maritime industry.

I was very close to Mum – born Jessica Pinfold – inevitably, because my father was away from home for long periods on naval duty. She played the piano and read to me and Euan a lot.

Her father, George Pinfold, was a Royal Navy engineering officer and later became the Conservative Mayor of Gillingham as well as being a member of the Magic Circle and Grand Master of the local Masonic Lodge. He was small and birdlike and had won various medals, including the British Empire Medal for service in the First World War. Euan and I were both very fond of Grandpa George – he used to pluck eggs and other objects from behind our ears and make coins disappear, and I remember sitting in the mayoral ceremonial chair with an enormous mayoral chain around my neck.

The circumstances of Grandpa's death were shocking. Mum never spoke about it, but as a 10-year-old boy I saw, as I sat on a train going to a dentist appointment, a newspaper with the headline 'Mayor of Gillingham murdered in bed by son'. George's stepson, Kenneth, had been diagnosed as a schizophrenic and had been in and out of mental institutions when George got him a labouring job in Chatham dock-yard. But the morning Kenneth was due to begin work, in February

1951, he grabbed a knife and stabbed his stepfather to death. Charged with attempted murder, he was found unfit to plead and was committed to a psychiatric asylum.

I kept my personal knowledge of the manner of Grandpa George's death entirely to myself for more than 40 years – until after Mum died in 1992. Pa then told Euan, who told me. The 'secret' was out in the open, but I told Euan I had always known the truth.

Later I gleaned some details of George's murder from a local newspaper account. George survived his stepson's assault long enough to give sworn evidence before a magistrate's court, specially convened, at his bedside in St Bartholomew's Hospital in the nearby town of Rochester.

As my 63-year-old grandfather lay on his deathbed, with a doctor leaning forward continually to moisten his lips, he told the magistrate that Kenneth had at first refused to get out of bed when called to begin his new job and then burst into George's bedroom. His testimony continued: 'I was lying in bed. My wife was resting her head on my right arm. He stabbed me in the abdomen. The wounds went deep. I got out of bed and closed with him. I was handicapped because the wounds he had inflicted were taking their toll on me.

'I managed to get the weapon from him at the top of the stairs. I went to the window and I threw the dagger into the front garden and called out for help.'

With the final moments of his life ticking away, my grandfather was shown a nine-inch dagger by a detective who asked if it was the weapon that had been used against him. George nodded in the affirmative, lay back on his pillows and passed away.

'There was hardly a more loved and respected person in the Medway Towns. Gillingham mourns its sailor mayor, so trusted for his good sense, wisdom and impartiality,' said Christopher Chavasse, the Bishop of Rochester, at Grandpa's funeral, attended by 12 Kent mayors and Admiral Sir Cecil Harcourt, Commander-in-Chief, The Nore, the senior Royal Navy officer responsible for protecting entrance to the port of London and merchant traffic along the east coast of Britain. Euan and I, however, were not present.

My grandfather on my father's side was called Joseph Ralph

Harper, and five generations of Joseph Ralph Harpers can be traced back to 1756, all in Rotherhithe on the River Thames in east London. Their occupations were respectively Engineer/Merchant, Artist/Sculptor, Engineer, Master Shipwright and Butcher/Beer Seller.

In 1904 Grandfather Harper went to Tientsin on the Shantung Peninsula in northeastern China to work for Lever Brothers Limited, then mainly a soap manufacturer but now an international conglomerate. Tientsin was a Treaty Port, 60 miles from Peking (now Beijing) where the big European powers all held 'Concessions' in which their own national laws reigned and which were defended by their own troops and local volunteers. Grandfather left Lever Brothers and set up his own import/export company, J.R. Harper & Co. In 1906 he was joined by his fiancée, Wilhelmina Hall, and they married in Shanghai Cathedral. Grandma Wilhelmina gave birth to six children, of which my Pa, Peter Harper, was the third.

Peter's first nine years of life were idyllic in a large happy family which spent holidays in its beach cottage at the resort of Peitaiho. Aged five, Pa began learning to play the piano while his education began at Tientsin Grammar School, which still exists and has a memorial inside the entrance inscribed 'To the Honoured Memory of Bertram Best-Dunkley, VC, Captain, Temp-Lieut Colonel, Lancashire Fusiliers. Assistant Master in this School.' It goes on to describe the deeds that won him his Victoria Cross as a 27-year-old leading attacks on German machine-gun positions on 17 August 1917 at Ypres, Belgium, resulting in wounds from which he died. The memorial was partially damaged by soldiers when Japan occupied northern China two decades later, but thankfully they gave up the task before it was comprehensively destroyed. At least two pupils of the school later became famous: the ballerina Margot Fonteyn and the writer and artist Mervyn Peake.

In 1920 Grandpa Harper took the entire family to the UK, where the three eldest boys were put into a boarding school, Rose Hill Preparatory in Sussex. The rest of the family returned to China and Pa did not see or hear from his father again until 1931. All communication was left to Grandma Wilhelmina.

During Grandpa's short absence in Britain, his British assistant fiddled the books at J.R. Harper & Co and he and a Chinese intermediary vanished, taking with them a large sum of money. Grandpa rushed back to China, worked to make the business recover and managed to keep paying school fees as his sons moved on to Bedford, one of the early British 'public schools'.

Pa excelled academically and at sport at Bedford. With his brothers he formed a jazz band, but his real love was for classical music, especially Mozart. On turning 18, his teachers were keen for him to go to Cambridge University, but the economic Great Depression of the 1930s was setting in and he felt obliged to get a job, becoming a Paymaster Cadet in the Royal Navy. By then, in China, trade had dried up, J.R. Harper & Co had gone bust and Grandpa took a job with the Tientsin City Water Works, of which he subsequently became managing director.

In 1931 Pa was appointed to a lovely new three-funnel County-class heavy cruiser HMS *Suffolk* and sailed for the China Station, which covered the coasts of China and its navigable rivers, the western part of the Pacific Ocean, and the waters around the then Dutch East Indies, now Indonesia. En route, in the Bay of Biscay, *Suffolk* passed her sister ship HMS *Cumberland*, and in an exchange of signals one said: 'It's a SUFFOLKing long way to China!'

During two years on the China Station Pa managed to wangle occasional leaves to visit his family in Tientsin. He returned to appointments in Portsmouth and then aboard the battlecruiser *Renown*, which was ordered at short notice into the Mediterranean in a vain attempt to bluff Italy out of invading Ethiopia in late 1935. This was frustrating for Pa because he had just met and fallen in love with the beautiful and then 23-year-old Jessica Pinfold. In 1936 he was posted overseas again, this time to HMS *Tamar*, the China Station's shore base in Hong Kong. He obtained permission to travel to the Far East by the Trans-Siberian Railway, again spending a leave with his family in Tientsin but not knowing it would be their last meeting until after the end of the Second World War.

Full-scale war broke out in July 1937 between Japan and China. Some 300,000 Chinese were massacred by their Japanese conquerors after the fall of Nanking in December 1937. The British business community was permitted to continue working until December 1941, but after the Japanese attack that month on the United States naval base at Pearl Harbor, Hawaii, they were interned as 'enemy aliens'. My grandparents and Auntie Dorea were herded with hundreds of others, including 300 children of Christian missionaries, into the Weihsien internment camp on the Shantung Peninsula and were there for four years. My Auntie Edie-Kay avoided their fate through friends in the Belgian Embassy who employed her as a children's nurse, giving her diplomatic immunity. She travelled with the Belgian family to South Africa and then to Cairo where she was employed by the American Red Cross.

Conditions in Weihsien – on the site of a former Presbyterian missionary school whose name in Chinese was 'Courtyard of the Happy Way' – were appalling. There was no privacy. Accommodation was overcrowded and squalid. The camp was surrounded by high walls, electrified wire, barbed wire and guard towers. Sanitation was unspeakable: there were 23 toilets for 1,800 people and there was no toilet paper. Extreme hunger and diarrhoea-related illnesses were constant. Bedding was infested with bugs.

Eric Liddell, the Tientsin-born Scottish athlete who won the 400 metres gold medal at the 1924 Paris Olympics, was one of the Weihsien internees. My Auntie Dorea was also the camp barber, and therefore cut Liddell's hair. Liddell had set a world record in his Olympic victory, but he withdrew from the 100 metres, his best event, at the Paris games because the final was due on a Sunday and his deep Christian principles prevented him from running on the Sabbath. His role in the 1924 Olympics and the events preceding the Games was portrayed in the film *Chariots of Fire*. Liddell's Scottish parents were missionaries in China, and he returned there after the Paris Olympics to become a minister of religion and begin missionary work himself.

It is funny how things turn up in one's own life. I read Liddell's life story many years ago and when I was teaching at Boroughmuir High School a call came to me from the casting director for *Chariots of Fire* asking if through Theatre Workshop, a community arts and culture project in Edinburgh, I could recruit some young girls as extras. Two of the important scenes in the film were shot in Edinburgh. The only remaining major cinder track in Scotland is at the Goldenacre sports ground which still has a 19th-century grandstand, so the 'Paris Olympics finals' were shot there. Another scene purporting to be in the Scottish church in Paris was shot in a church just off Edinburgh's Broughton Street.

Liddell was also a rugby union international, playing seven times for his country before returning to China. He died in Weihsien, malnourished and aged just 43, from an inoperable brain tumour just five months before the camp was liberated. He was much loved for his gentle personality and the games and races he organised for the children. Another popular inmate was a Trappist monk who was caught smuggling 150 eggs into the compound under the prison wire. Sentenced to 45 days in solitary, he took the punishment lightly, insisting that as a monk he was used to long and lonely meditations.

At the time of Pearl Harbor, two of Pa's brothers were in Singapore. Bob, the eldest, was in the Malay States Police and after the British surrender to the Japanese was interned in the notorious Changi Jail where he looked after pigs at the prison farm. He survived four years of extreme privation and continued in the Malay Police after the war, serving in the 1947–1960 Malayan Emergency, which was in all but name a war against communist insurgents, and reaching the rank of Commissioner. Brian, the youngest, and the twin of Auntie Edie-Kay, was a young pilot officer in the RAF. His unit managed to escape from Singapore, before Japanese forces arrived, aboard a ship carrying rice for Australia but was captured by the rapidly advancing Japanese when the ship put into an Indonesian port. As a prisoner of war, Brian was forced to break rocks building airstrips, enduring starvation and brutality and watching comrades die. He became an architect in Australia after the war.

Pa's eldest brother, Ralph, was back in the UK as an officer in the Second Battalion Hertfordshire Regiment. By the time of D-Day, 6 June 1944, he was the colonel of the regiment given the task of capturing and holding the beach near Ver-sur-Mer, a small Normandy village. He was successful and forged a strong relationship with the local mayor. A memorial to Uncle Ralph's regiment was erected in the village and today a road named 'Avenue Colonel J.R. Harper' runs through it down to the sea.

On liberation from Weihsien by American troops in August 1945 my grandparents' hopes of recovering their property were dashed as civil war swept through China between Mao Zedong's communist Red Army and the Kuomintang Nationalist forces under Chiang Kai-Shek. In 1946 they were forced to flee and as they went down a river in a small boat communist and nationalist forces were engaged in battle from opposite banks. They cowered in the saloon as bullets flew and subsequently found several lodged in their meagre luggage. On arriving, destitute, in Britain, they lived with one of Grandma Harper's sisters in Streatham, south London. Grandpa died soon after from long untreated diabetes but Grandma survived until 1969. Although increasingly blind and crippled, she had perfect recall of names and places and regaled visitors with amusing stories of old China. During her final years she was lovingly cared for by her daughter, my Auntie Dorea, who was by then the landlady of the Anchor Inn in the village of Sidlesham in West Sussex. While both Euan and I were working in different parts of Africa, she died peacefully sitting in her armchair with the pub cat asleep on her lap.

6

The new Parliament and the Three Musketeers

In Scotland's new Parliament I was depicted as having added a 'daub of theatricality to the often drab proceedings of Scottish politics.'[1] My 'Dr Who' scarf and fedora helped get me classified as a unique parliamentary species by political journalists who were clearly bemused by the appearance of a relatively mild-mannered teacher approaching retirement age in the maelstrom of the new body politic. They were agog when they discovered that I often eschewed political rhetoric and read poems to inspire my Green supporters.

They probably wondered how I was going to survive. Twelve years later, maybe they were still wondering!

There was a huge amount of interest initially in my private life, which Jenny understandably found quite intrusive. I was filmed playing the piano, photographed ironing my shirts and cooking bread and butter pudding, and my little nursery in my back garden of oak seed saplings, which I planted out in woods, schools and housing estates, received a lot of attention. The publicity and intrusiveness did not bother me. The photographers were very professional and the majority of the journalists were genuinely interested in finding out what made me tick rather than attempting to portray me as some kind of weird eccentric. I think I managed to disguise my real eccentricities quite successfully, and as time has gone on I think we have managed to persuade most people that our Green policies are just as interesting as the party personalities.

Before getting down to parliamentary work, I needed to report back at Boroughmuir High School, where I had taught for the past 17 years and

[1] Alan Taylor, writing in the *Sunday Herald*, 11 March 2007.

where I was assistant head of the modern studies department. I said I would be happy to serve three months' notice but that, frankly, I would be unable to give full attention to the job. Since an experienced teacher, an old friend of mine, had already begun substituting for me, I suggested that I be allowed to resign immediately. This was accepted: it felt quite wounding and inappropriate, nonetheless, not least because it allowed no time for me to say goodbye to my classes. I did at least receive a fantastic reception in the staff room when I popped in on the first working day after the election: my colleagues all stood and cheered and shook my hand. It felt as though I had come back with soccer's World Cup!

One of my first tasks in my new life was to recruit two permanent staff with the £35,000 allowance permitted me under the rules. More than 300 people applied for the jobs. A panel that included business-people and journalists, but no Green Party members, interviewed six finalists for each post. I sat at the side, observed the interviews and commented at the end. When Alison Johnson, an applicant for office manager, left the room the entire panel looked at me and smiled, and one said: 'She'll keep you in order.' He was right. She has done. Alison, a Scottish international runner at 800 metres and an athletics coach, has been with me for the whole of my parliamentary career.

Steve Burgess, an Edinburgh University scientist and a Greenpeace activist, became my researcher. I remembered just before he was interviewed that Steve had been one of my guitar pupils when he was aged eight years. He subsequently took up the violin and plays now with several fiddle groups.

Alison's and Steve's first eight years of work with me were rewarded in 2007 when both were elected to Edinburgh Council as Green Party councillors, although neither of them had been a member of the party when I recruited them to my staff. Alison's superb council work was recognised when the party selected her to represent it at the fourth Scottish Parliament election, scheduled for 2011, at the top of the Edinburgh and Lothians regional list.

*   *   *

As a one-man band, albeit with huge support from Steve and Alison, the reality was that the only power I had in Parliament was that of reasoned argument. I knew I would have to use the platform to the utmost of my ability, working my socks off both inside and outside the assembly.

My goals were to change the mindsets of the key players in the big parties and to wage such a dynamic and sustained campaign that Green Party parliamentary representation would multiply at the next Scottish Parliament elections.

I was not a lone maverick in the Parliament. Thanks to the PR element of the election, two other nonconformists had been elected – the colourful Scottish Socialist Tommy Sheridan[2] and the Labour rebel Denis Canavan who stood as an independent. Our impact as 'Three Musketeers' developed out of all proportion to our numerical strength.

In the first few months of the new Parliament's life, Tommy's staff were frequent visitors to my office, constantly trying to woo me into a Red-Green alliance which I resisted with great determination. I had no intention of confusing those who gave us their votes into thinking that they had voted for anything other than the Green Party. Tommy was a master of spin, and once he had plonked himself down in the middle of the Three Musketeers' allocated seats, with Canavan and me on either side, he proved impossible to dislodge, ensuring that he was centre stage whenever the TV or film cameras swung in our direction. I blame the slight deafness in my left ear on four years of sitting next to Tommy's verbal blasts.

Thanks again to the two-vote system, the 1999 election produced a hung Parliament. No party had won an absolute majority, and the reality was that no one knew what should happen next. No script existed for coalition government in Britain: there were no precedents to consult. 'Welcome to the world of continental politics, where government is not about winning and losing, but about complex and continuing negotiations with other parties,' observed one journalist. 'British commentators affect to disdain the European coalition-style of politics as

---

[2] Tommy Sheridan was imprisoned for three years on 26 January 2011 on a charge of perjury. Following the longest perjury trial in Scottish history, a jury concluded he had lied in court to win £200,000 damages against a Sunday newspaper, the *News of the World*.

slightly backward, but in reality it is Britain that is behind the times.'[3]

In the end, the Labour Party, with 56 of the 129 seats, formed a coalition government with the fourth-biggest party, the Scottish Liberal Democrats, who had won 17 seats. Politics in Scotland now reflected reality more than politics at Westminster. First-past-the-post elections create artificial majorities, implying seismic shifts in public attitudes which have not really happened. One major outcome of the Scottish Parliament vote was that we, the new parliamentarians of Scotland, became aware that the rest of Britain would be watching what happened at Holyrood to see if electoral reform should be extended to Westminster. The issue was like a slow-fuse time-bomb which exploded with great force further south 11 years later when the Conservative Party won a first-past-the-post-only general election, but without a clear majority, forcing it into a historic coalition government with the Liberal Democrats.

I was also acutely aware that my personal conduct would be closely observed. As Britain's first Green Party parliamentarian I represented an important cause whose supporters' rationale went totally unheard at Westminster. It was not in my nature to be abusive, so although I recognised the need for robust political debate I was determined to be civil and polite at all times. It was not really very much different from being a teacher. After all, in my modern studies classes I had for years encouraged my students to analyse politicians' misrepresentation, exaggerations and economies with the truth.

I attended more debates in that first Parliament than in either of the succeeding ones because I found that there were quite a few MSPs who were happy to take interventions from me. I usually only intervened when I was trying to get a Green view across and in a way that I hoped would be helpful to the development of the debate. What Tommy Sheridan probably did not realise was that I was secretly competing with him throughout those first four years to make the highest number of contributions to debates. I think I beat him by about 20 with extra effort on the home straight in March 2003, by when we had both been name-checked in the parliamentary record more than 1,400 times each.

[3] Ian Macwhirter, 'Now the battle starts for the hearts and minds of a nation,' *Sunday Herald*, 9 May 1999.

7

My 'Kim time'

When I was aged six the family moved from the magic of Orkney to the inner suburbs of London. My father had been posted as a naval attaché to the Cabinet Office and then the Ministry of Defence, where one of his daily tasks was to help Emmanuel 'Manny' Shinwell, the former Red Clydesider who had become Secretary of State for War in the post-war Labour government, to remove his overcoat and help him put it on again. Pa also did a lot of hush-hush work which some time later earned him an OBE.

I was sent ahead of the family from Orkney to Bedhampton, a boarding prep school near Portsmouth. I can't pretend that I was anything other than deeply unhappy. My Auntie Dorea accompanied me by train the thousand miles to Bedhampton. She kept telling me not to cry as I sat gazing miserably out of the compartment window at the passing towns and countryside.

During all my time at Bedhampton I suffered from nocturnal enuresis, or bed-wetting, the unintentional passing of urine while asleep. No one knew at that time that the condition resulted from a late development of the sphincter in the urinary tract. It was thought – not least by Miss Brierley, Bedhampton's terrifying headmistress – that small children could be persuaded, or frightened, into not wetting their beds. From bitter experience I know that no matter how many times a child says, 'I didn't mean it', grown-ups behave as though he or she is doing it on purpose.

Miss Brierley ordered my house mistress to make me wash my own sheets every time I wet the bed, which was frequently. She was the bane of my life. On one occasion she punished me by putting me in an isolation dorm with another child who had also incurred her wrath.

40

We made the mistake of talking after lights out. Miss Brierley crashed into the room and leaned over us. I could just make out her contorted face in the shaft of light from the open door as she hissed at me: 'You're not going to talk any more, are you?' I was completely confused about how to answer a negative statement followed by a positive interrogative. I was terrified and cannot remember whether I replied 'yes' or 'no'. Whichever answer I gave was wrong as far as she was concerned because, without being given a chance to explain myself, she thrashed me with a cane.

I was fascinated from an early age by machines, engines, aeroplanes and the building of houses. My mother told me that when I was three she found me bailing out the toilet bowl with the soap dish to try to find out where the water went. A teacher at Bedhampton knew of my interests and kindly arranged for his brother to take me to a building site to see how a house was built. I was really excited and went off in high spirits and can even now remember the atmosphere amidst the bricks being laid and the noise of the hoists. But something scared me – I can no longer recall what – and I was taken back to Bedhampton and was made to stand in front of the whole school while the dreaded Miss Brierley berated me for bringing shame on the institution by spurning the generosity of the teacher's young brother. The horrid cold feeling at the complete unfairness of life remains a vivid memory.

I never communicated my Bedhampton problems to my parents or my brother Euan, who also went to the school. To this day I do not understand why my parents sent either of us to boarding school at such young ages. Much later Euan discovered that my mother had spent some time in hospital after the war with gynaecological problems. She was probably also suffering from depression, which would have made it difficult to cope largely on her own with two boisterous young children. I know that I was regarded as a difficult child who had to be kept on reins and who was prone to temper tantrums – and I do remember once tearing up the family ration book which caused considerable angst. Another factor was that most military families at that time sent their children to boarding schools, and it was probably perfectly logical for Pa and Mum to take advantage of the available subsidy.

Although my parents did not know the cause, they were aware of my deep unhappiness at Bedhampton and consequently brought me home to London, a rented flat just round the corner from EMI's Abbey Road studios where The Beatles would record their 1960s hits. I was first sent to a funny little private school just off Baker Street. The kids were awfully posh and I was taught knitting as well as maths. My parents moved me to a state primary school, Barrowhill in St John's Wood, near Lord's Cricket Ground, where, to my mother's horror, I began to talk with a Cockney accent. Barrowhill was almost something out of Dickens. It had gaslights, which I was permitted to light as the gaslight monitor. There were ink wells and dipping pens, and although we hardly saw the much-feared head teacher we knew he was handy with the cane.

Walks home with Euan, who was also removed from boarding school, were enlivened by opportunities to play in and explore the many bomb sites that littered post-war London. Heaps of rubble with a profusion of flowers and tree saplings were exciting wildernesses that had an extraordinary attraction: they were our little kingdom. One bomb site was next to the Grand Central line north from Marylebone Station. A train carrying all manner of electrical equipment had been hit by a German bomb and the material had been thrown off the track throughout the site. We collected microphones, gyros and yards of copper wire that we took home to become playthings.

*   *   *

An enchanting new time began in 1949 when Pa was appointed as supply commander on the cruiser HMS *Mauritius*, which sailed for a tour in the East Indies based at Trincomalee in Ceylon, now Sri Lanka. Mum, Euan and I sailed east by troopship. My brother and I were pupils at the ship's school during the six weeks at sea. Otherwise I ran my Hornby train set on top of the lifeboat lockers by day and was delighted when we went ashore in Egypt by the sleight of hand of the gully-gully men who produced live chicks from behind our ears. At night I leaned on the salt-encrusted wooden taffrail at the ship's stern, or rear, and marvelled at the sea's phosphorescence and the magnificent ceiling of stars. Out there, far beyond our tiny world, not a square inch of the heavens was without a mix of millions, maybe billions, of bright winking diamonds and pinpoints of light. I have never since seen skies to compare with those above the Red Sea and Indian Ocean.

On arrival in Colombo, Ceylon's capital, we stayed in the legendary colonial Galle Face Hotel facing the Indian Ocean. It was reputed to be the oldest hotel east of Suez. The tropical air was redolent with perfume of frangipani and other flowers and our Burmese teak-floored rooms were unimaginably large. I fell asleep to the sound of the ceaseless crash of waves on the shore.

A huge 4-litre Humber Hawk staff car, with a Royal Navy driver, picked us up. I sank into the leather seats as we travelled the 165 miles eastwards across the jungle-covered centre of Ceylon to our new home in Trincomalee, the port city on the east coast whose natural deep-water harbour – the fifth largest in the world – had attracted seafarers like Marco Polo, Ptolemy, and traders from China since ancient times. The British captured Trincomalee, fondly known as Trinco, from the Dutch in 1795 – Horatio Nelson described the harbour as the most magnificent he had seen – and held it until Ceylon's independence in 1948. During the Second World War it was the Home Port of the Eastern Fleet of the Royal Navy, which maintained a base there until 1957.

I used to wander like Kipling's Kim among saffron-robed Buddhist monks through bazaars piled with spices and freshly caught fish, dodging tame elephants and emaciated cattle. I was a right little colonialist, a child of that time, spending my annas and rupees in little bazaar kiosks on colonial stamps. My brother and I were in the open air nearly all the time, even during the monsoon. As the clouds above opened up, we would stand still and let ourselves be drenched by warm rain and watch waters gushing down the storm drains leading to the beach in front of our house. Then as the clouds moved on we marvelled at the steam, scents and smells rising from the soaked earth.

I turned nut brown under the sun and collected sea shells along the soft white coral sand of Nilaweli on the Bay of Bengal, where naval families held beach parties and tested their skills on the surfing waves. I still have a box of those lovely shells to reminisce over. I was not to discover for another 40 years that while I was playing happily on Trinco's beaches my future wife, Jenny, was being born just to the north of me across the Bay of Bengal in Calcutta.

I tried to surf only once, fell off the board and was turned over and over uncontrollably as though in a washing machine. I felt rather silly when I found myself lying bruised in six inches of water still trying to fight my way to the surface. I contented myself after that with diving into the waves after they had spent most of their energy and have never since tried to surf.

Ironically, in view of my surfing failure, I worked with surfers at three successive Scottish Parliament elections. Surfers Against Sewage is an energetic environmental campaign group with a mission to rid the UK coastline of sewage. During the 1999 campaign it persuaded me and David Bellamy, the British broadcaster and environmental campaigner, to sit on a six feet-long inflated brown plastic 'turd' to illustrate the problem on many of Britain's beaches. The history of Surfers Against Sewage is typical of many 'green' organisations. Surfing in Cornwall, Chris Hines came out of a wave with a panty liner stuck to the back of his head and a human turd squished between his chest and his surfboard. He had simply had enough. He said he and his fellow surfers ingested sewage, breathed it in and became ill with gastroenteritis and ear and throat infections. Hines was outraged by then Prime Minister Margaret Thatcher's categorical assertions that all sewage in the UK was treated before it was discharged. 'We were well aware that 400 million gallons of raw sewage were being discharged every day into the sea,' said Hines, who launched Surfers Against Sewage in 1990 with two other core members. They perfected the art of media-friendly stunts – such as the giant turd. They also wore gas masks with their wetsuits to spread the word that their playground was seriously polluted. Twenty years ago Hines and his activists were dismissed as 'meddling hippies', and a threat to Britain's beach resorts. Two decades later, even the Queen has celebrated their success in cleaning up hundreds of miles of coastline: in 2008 she awarded Hines an MBE for services to the environment.

Forsaking Nilaweli's waves, I learned to swim instead in the calm, vast and deep waters of the harbour where, in the transparent blue-green sea, I could see down clearly some 10 metres and watched turtles, giant rays and shoals of gleaming, luminous fish. Every few days BOAC flying boats on the Britain-Australia route touched down in the harbour.

The first bungalow we lived in was called Tigh-na-Mara, or By The Sea, outside the naval base. The shower room was a concrete box that was home to a family of toads, which we tolerated happily. But Pa, as a senior officer, later inherited Chelsburgh, a larger house near the dockyard gate, the Anglican church, the officers' club and the harbour swimming area. We had two servants, Manuel, a Tamil, and Savara, a lovely gentle Sinhalese Buddhist whose face was ravaged by appalling smallpox scars.

School was a tiny primary school for Royal Navy officers' children. Mrs Modder, a big and colourful Sinhalese, was the headmistress. She had her own private zoo. I was taught maths by a fantastic 24-year-old Englishman, an Oxford graduate, who got me to zoom ahead in mathematics, helping me master algebra, calculus and Euclidian geometry. A young navy doctor who was a passionate botanist and zoologist used to take me on walks along the shore and in the forested area around the harbour. I will never forget discovering with him a sea slug the size of a small melon, observing it for half an hour and prodding it with a stick to watch how its defence mechanisms worked. I also found a cowrie shell that is quite the most beautiful object I have ever seen and which remains in my collection of objects from the past.

While Trinco was hot and steamy, the Royal Navy had an airy retreat upcountry in the cool hills around Kandy, where we swam in crystal pools among forests and lush tea gardens fecund with beautiful butterflies, exotic coloured birds, strange insects and snakes. In Ceylon my appreciation of the beauty of nature, first aroused on windswept Orkney, matured and deepened.

Every other day we would board the Navy's Bedford bus, painted in faded blue with a big RN in white on its side and with an extra-ordinary music-like gearbox, and be driven to local sites – waterfalls, tea plantations, the elephant parade in Kandy, the Temple of the Golden Tooth, and calm white temples with golden gleaming minarets. Euan and I explored freely beyond the villa. We once stumbled across a huge snake. It looked like a python, but was more probably a cobra. Happily it seemed not to be bothered by us because it had its head up a storm drain. That made no difference to us. We took off like startled rabbits and did not stop running until we got back to the villa.

My parents took a holiday in Singapore half way through our time in Trinco to see Pa's second oldest brother Bob, the Malaya-based police commissioner, and his younger sister Dorea, visiting Singapore. Mum went out by troopship to join Pa who had already arrived there courtesy of a Royal Air Force Sunderland flying boat. Mum, I learned years later, had an embarrassing experience as the ship began to manoeuvre through the passages between the many small islands leading to Singapore's main harbour. A very young army officer had fallen passionately in love with her on the voyage and when she rejected his latest advance he threw himself overboard. Happily, he was rescued from an unnecessarily early watery grave.

Dad was absent from Trinco for long periods aboard HMS *Mauritius*. Among *Mauritius*' duties was visiting all the dependencies around the Indian Ocean which had supported Britain during the Second World War and entertaining dignitaries there. Watching *Mauritius* steam into harbour and drop anchor at the end of a mission, with the crew lined up in white tropical uniforms under awnings on the aft-deck with a big ceremonial rum barrel, was deeply romantic. A daily rum ration was issued for 315 years to all enlisted Royal Navy sailors, even those in nuclear submarines, until 1970. Rum consumption must have inspired the 200-year-old sea shanty 'What Shall We Do With the Drunken Sailor?', one of whose refrains goes: 'Sling him in the longboat till he's sober.' Years later, when on an airmen's course in Nuneaton as a Sea Cadet, I learned how dangerous this custom could be. The gloom that hung over the air station was explained as having been the consequence of two young naval airmen, twins, being given 'sippers' of everybody else's rum on their eighteenth birthday: they both died of alcohol poisoning.

Cocktail parties and raucous gatherings galore followed the arrival

46

in Trinco of any Royal Navy ship. Pa used to entertain on the piano –
Chopin waltzes, Tom Lehrer ditties and Fats Waller songs. Guests
danced to music from a huge wind-up gramophone that I inherited.
On special occasions I still play old jazz 78s on it. Everybody smoked.
Senior Service cigarettes were sold in 50-packs to sailors at knock-
down duty-free prices. There were no health warnings on the packets
in those days, and non-smokers were in the minority. They were issued
to serving men and they were known as 'blue-liners' because they had
a faint blue line running the length of the cigarette to discourage black
marketeering, for which there were severe penalties. Euan and I used
to get up early to scour through the debris of the previous night's
celebrations. Glasses and ashtrays were full of cigarette stubs. I picked
up half-smoked fag ends and sneaked away to smoke them, and it got
me into a habit later that I struggled to kick for more than 30 years. I
was in my 40s when I decided to stop smoking and have not touched a
cigarette since.

Dad was away for long periods during our Ceylon years. I only
learned much later that *Mauritius* was one of the ships blockading
Iran following the nationalisation by Prime Minister Mohammad
Mosaddegh of the British-owned Anglo-Iranian Oil Company, later
British Petroleum or BP. The blockade reduced Iran's oil income to
almost zero over a period of about three years. MI6 and the CIA
eventually plotted Mosaddegh's removal from power in a military
coup in August 1953.

It was in Trinco also that I learned how irresponsible men can be.
Sober Island, in the great harbour, had a cemetery for seamen who had
died in Trinco down the centuries – from cholera and dysentery or
falling from the rigging of the old sailing ships. When ordinary seamen
had shore leave they often spent a few days camping on Sober Island
and we would go with them. The ratings carried .303 Lee Enfield
rifles, and we were appalled when after a day spent swimming and
sailing they began shooting the Hanging Parrots which flocked and
foraged in the island's trees, hanging upside down from branches to
reach fruits and flowers. Mainly green, but with splashes of red, blue,
yellow and orange feathers, they were blasted to bits by the rifle shells.
It was my first experience of people cavalierly shooting beautiful wild

creatures just for the 'fun' of it. I know it reinforced still more strongly my love for natural creation.

I felt dreadfully sad the day we left Trinco for ever. We took the overnight train to Colombo, and as it pulled out of the station to chunter westwards a lone piper played a lament. Ceylon was then a peaceful country, so beautiful that some early explorers thought it must have been where Paradise was located. Many decades later I found it impossible to comprehend that Trinco, lying on the border between the Tamil north and Sinhalese south, had become too dangerous to visit because it was at the heart of the 26-year Sri Lankan civil war that ended in May 2009. In peace, Trinco was a shining example for Ceylon/Sri Lanka's ethnic diversity. It had ethnic Buddhist Sinhalese and Hindu Tamils in equal numbers, as well as a large population of Muslims. But Trinco no longer knew peace and among the atrocities perpetrated there were the brutal executions of schoolboys on the beautiful beaches where I had once roamed.

Our troopship home, the *Empire Orwell*, was packed with squaddies returning from their national service in the war against the communists in Malaya. Our bit of the ship was divided from theirs by steel wires drawn so tight that it looked as though it was possible to balance and walk along them. Testing my own tightrope skills, I lost balance and fell on the army side, snapping the two bones of my right forearm, the radius and ulna, clean in two. I am sure I made a lot of noise when I saw I had an extra wrist joint. A soldier whisked me down to the sick bay to be treated by a young army doctor who had never set a bone in his life. There was no quick-setting plaster of paris on board, so my arm was encased in an improvised splint made of wooden slats and yards and yards of cotton bandaging. When we got to London I was taken to Paddington Hospital where they unwound the bandaging, took an x-ray and put on a proper plaster. I've never been able to rotate my right hand properly since.

8

Down to work. Getting into Parliament is the Green Party's best possible publicity stunt

The Green Party had battled for the hearts and minds of voters in the first Scottish Parliament election. Now, as Parliament convened for the first time on 1 July 1999, I had to try to earn the respect of my fellow parliamentarians.

I recognised that I had more chance of getting our ideas across if I adopted a consensual rather than a confrontational approach and have pursued that policy ever since. Friends in other parties said I was being 'too nice' to be a successful politician in the parliamentary rough and tumble. I took this as a compliment rather than a criticism. The fact was that I had rarely been a rabble-rouser. I had always believed in being courteous and polite, advancing ideas through thoughtful dialogue. A leading political journalist asked me why I was not making 'a nuisance of myself'.[1] I told him about advice I had been given long ago: 'The best thing you can do in politics, Robin, is to be yourself, because if you're not you'll soon be found out.' And the truth was that much of my philosophy of life had been shaped – and remains shaped – by the simple teachings of the New Testament, and especially by Paul's First Epistle to the Corinthians, which in chapter 13 famously begins: 'If I speak in the tongues of men and of angels, but have not love, I am only a resounding gong or a clanging cymbal.' And ends: 'And now abideth faith, hope and love. But the greatest of these is love' – words that are set in brass letters in the Scots vernacular, as translated by William Laughton Lorimer, in the paving

[1] 'Self-Reliant Robin', by Douglas Fraser, *The Sunday Herald*, 10 March 2002.

of the entrance to Queensbury House, part of the Scottish Parliament complex. I quoted this Lorimer translation in my speech to the Queen on the occasion of the opening of the purpose-built new Scottish Parliament building, designed by the Catalan architect Enric Miralles, on 9 October 2004.[2]

The political journalist also wrote: 'There is something almost childlike about Harper, a gee-whiz boyishness. But don't let that or the eccentricity deceive you. There is a real seriousness about him.' Modesty does not inhibit me from quoting that writer!

I risk, however, depicting myself as some kind of goody-goody. I have given speeches designed to rouse the feelings of large numbers of people, and it is a heady experience and scarily thrilling when you pitch a speech that successfully fires up supporters on the hustings or at a rally. It can be dangerous, however, with Adolf Hitler's speeches at the Nuremberg rallies, amounting to mass brainwashing, as an extreme example.

I remember at the end of a CND march along Edinburgh's Princes Street hearing one of the more experienced orators whipping up emotions against the police and calling for the march to move to the nearest police station because, we were told, ONE person had been arrested by what was said to be a snatch squad at the back of the march. My turn to speak came immediately after and I said I had been a member of CND for nearly 40 years, that I was marching for peace, and that the movement had a history of peaceful cooperation with the police, not least because they protected us against descent into the kind of civil disorder that could destroy the aims of our marches on the occasions when small groups of agitators pursued their own agendas. I have no idea how effective my speech was, but I do know that only a very small group of people eventually made a desultory protest outside the police station.

*   *   *

[2] The passage reads in Lorimer's Scots vernacular version: "*Gin I speak wi the tungs o men an angels, but hae nae luve i my hairt, I am no nane better nor dunnerin bress or a rínging cymbal . . . There is three things bides for ey: faith, howp, luve. But the grytest o the three is luve.*"

Getting into Parliament had been our best possible publicity stunt. In the weeks that followed nearly all the publicity centred on my personal election as the first and lone Green rather than what the party I represented stood for. Because I had no real 'power' I decided my role had to be to prick consciences, to make other members of the Parliament think about green issues. I kept in mind the aphorism: even a flea landing on an elephant's backside can make the elephant change direction. They would only respond if I was constructive, if my style was moderate even if my ideas were radical. My fellow parliamentarians also needed to see that I accepted the reality that I was in a minority of one and was ready, whenever necessary, to reconcile principle with pragmatism. I was prepared to compromise, perhaps more than most within the party.

Analysts warned that the better I performed the more other major parties would take on environmental issues as their own and squeeze out the Greens. As far as I was concerned, the greener other parties became the better. I had always fought on principle, not to have some glittering political career. And I knew that however much of our agenda others appropriated, there would always be a case for a Green Party. The desperately slow progress in addressing climate change by mainline politicians everywhere on the planet makes this even truer today than it was back in 1999.

The Green message had also to go beyond Parliament, because we wanted to increase our representation at Holyrood come the second Scottish election scheduled for 2003. Therefore, I accepted every invitation to visit or speak – conferences, universities, colleges, schools, small local communities. I criss-crossed Scotland from Kirkcudbright to Kirkwall and from Aberdeen to Arran. I planted oak saplings from my garden nursery. I opened community recycling projects and visited environmental endeavours of all kinds. I spoke about the issues I wanted to raise in Parliament – renewable energy, waste recycling, genetically modified crops, tourism, sustainable fishing, house insulation and anything at all I was asked to speak about. I was rarely offered fees or even expenses, and when I was I refused them. Contributions, however, to my favourite charity, ChildLine, were always welcomed as an alternative.[3] I received many 'Dear Mr Harper' letters following these visits, mainly from children. They were largely kind, and sometimes unwittingly funny – such as one that arrived from an 11-year-old boy after I had given a talk to children at a primary school about waste recycling. It began: 'Dear Mr Harper, Thank you for talking rubbish . . .'

The moment I moved outside the regional constituency from which I was elected – Edinburgh and the Lothians – I received no parliamentary expenses. At the same time, I was giving more than 20 per cent of my salary, some £500 a month rising to £600, to the party. Indeed, without my salary contribution the party would not have had any money in the bank. Although we had received tens of thousands of votes in the 1999 election the Green Party had barely 500 paid-up members.

One of the advantages I had over parliamentarians from mainstream parties was that I was very obviously 'different'. There were periods when I was on radio and TV so often that it felt almost non-stop. I was freer to speak on anything at all because I was not 'whipped', and on screen I always wore a green or brightly coloured tie.

Throughout that first Parliament I was clearly indispensable to the party, so I had to be on my very best behaviour, living by our principles as much as possible as well as preaching them. I was determined to try to be the 'lowest cost parliamentarian'. I was the only parliamentarian who was offered and refused a parking space at Holyrood. I either walk to work, or take the bus.

I had to watch my alcohol intake. There were lots of receptions and cross-party meetings where wine was served. It was difficult to say no, so I set myself a strict limit of a glass at each get-together. This was not always easy to stick to!

I worked flat-out until something blew and then I would take a day or two off to recover. I was often completely physically exhausted, although I continued to run marathons in the first few years until I was past 60.

[3] ChildLine is a free 24-hour counselling service for children and young people up to 18. It deals with any issue which causes distress or concern, such as child abuse, bullying and sex.

I had decided always to treat members of the general public who telephoned or emailed me as people who possibly had voted Green and who therefore had a very specific call on my services. Some of it was pretty humdrum, but there was also much that excited me, especially at the small local community level, where humble projects of great importance escape news headlines. I tried to keep in mind constantly the splendid Louis de Bernières[4] aphorism: 'The ultimate truth is that history ought to consist only of the anecdotes of the little people who are caught up in it.'

One of my proudest early invitations was to open a small community sewage treatment plant at Watten, a village of 320 souls seven miles south of Thurso where I was born. The villagers had got together with Scottish Water, the public corporation providing water and sewerage services, and the Scottish Environment Protection Agency (SEPA), the country's environmental regulator, and devised their own project to replace septic tanks and conform to European Union regulations, returning all the water they used to the local burn in pristine condition. It is a small plant with a series of Archimedes Screws aerating the muck and filtering out pure water from the remaining sludge. The plant needs no employees. The water quality is monitored every three hours by computer. If infectious agents reach a certain critical level, the computer sends a warning signal to the SEPA headquarters in Stirling 200 miles away.

It went unnoticed in the rest of the world, but it was a big day in Watten! Scottish Water put up a plaque which read: 'This sewage treatment plant was opened by Robin Harper etc.' All the kids from the local primary school were there. Whenever I'm invited to open a garden or eco-project it is very important to involve children whenever possible – with their parents' permission, of course. At Watten I selected the tiniest one to help me pull the tasselled cord that unveiled the plaque.

---

[4] Author of *Captain Corelli's Mandolin* and *Birds Without Wings*.

9

Back to London and then Scotland

Returning to London from Ceylon in 1951, we reclaimed our house at 9 Hill Road in St John's Wood. Euan and I settled back at Barrowhill Primary School where I prepared for the key eleven-plus public examination. Mum set about making friends while Pa was posted to the Royal Navy Air Station *Yeovilton*, near the Somerset town of Yeovil, as the base supply commnder. Royal Navy Seafires, basically Spitfires with an arrester hook bolted beneath the tail for landing on aircraft carriers, operated from *Yeovilton* together with ancient Fairey Firefly fighter-bombers. Pa seemed to be happy there. He made many flights, played lots of cricket and frequently entertained the wardroom with his piano playing.

Mum, Euan and I joined Pa in Somerset during the Easter and summer holidays, staying in a country house hotel in a small village called Charlton Mackrell. Euan and I wandered the lush local meadows and played in and dammed the streams that ran through the hotel grounds. We used to walk on the local downs and delight in the local train, known as The Bucket, consisting of a little tank engine and one carriage, puffing its way along the valley between Yeovil and Taunton.

Everything changed again in 1951 when Pa flew to Malta to join the Glasgow-built aircraft carrier HMS *Ocean* bound for Sasebo, one of Japan's most important naval harbours just 110 miles south of Korea. We did not see him again for two years. Sasebo was the base for Royal Navy and U.S. Navy ships throughout the war between South and North Korea that took some three million lives. *Ocean*'s Fireflies, designed before the outbreak of the Second World War, were tasked with bombing support activities over the front lines, mainly disrupting

North Korean and Chinese enemy communications, including transport network tunnels, bridges and supply bunkers. *Ocean* also carried a squadron of Hawker Sea Furies, the last propeller-driven fighters to serve with the Royal Navy, to provide cover for the Fireflies. Fleet Air Arm pilot Lieutenant Peter 'Hoagy' Carmichael downed a Soviet Union-built MiG-15 jet fighter in air-to-air combat over Korea, making the Sea Fury one of the few prop-driven fighter aircraft to shoot down a jet-powered fighter.

While Pa's pilot comrades, whom he debriefed, flew hundreds of dangerous sorties in the Korean War, deaths were largely caused by accidents on the deck of the aircraft carrier in heavy seas and strong winds

When *Ocean* returned from Korea we went to Plymouth and stood on Plymouth Hoe – where Sir Francis Drake is reputed to have played his famous game of bowls in 1588 before sailing out with the English fleet to engage with the Spanish Armada – to watch Pa's ship glide into harbour, her paying-off pennant streaming from the masthead. All across the harbour hooters and sirens screamed, ships' bells clanged and bosuns' whistles piped in welcome. When the terrific din began to subside we could hear *Ocean*'s Royal Marine band, marching along the flight deck and back playing Hearts of Oak, the official march of the Royal Navy, while the rest of the crew lined the sides of the ship in their 'Number Ones', their best ceremonial uniforms. It was very stirring and strengthened my desire to make a future career in the Royal Navy.

While Pa was away I passed my eleven-plus and went on to St Marylebone Grammar School. It was only six years after the end of World War Two, and many of the teachers were very old or were ex-servicemen who, in some cases, clearly had no qualifications. The head teacher's attitude to discipline was draconian. Bullying was institutional. Even prefects were allowed to administer corporal punishment, unheard of in most other English grammar schools at that time. The ritual involved stretching the offender on the long table in the prefects' room and belabouring his rear end with a gym shoe. First years were forced to run the gauntlet of jeering third and second years in a tunnel that ran from the pupils' entrance into the tiny square of asphalt which served as a playground. Anyone who reacted to the pushing and shoving was taken down some steps to an area outside the boiler room and beaten up. First years had to wear their school caps pulled down over their eyes and as your age increased the angle increased until when you were a sixth year you could wear it perched on the very back of your head or not at all.

Happily all this was swept away when a new head teacher, Harold Llewellyn Smith, was appointed in 1954. He put an immediate stop to the bullying and brought in some new young teachers. Inspired by Mum, who like Pa was an accomplished pianist, I learned to play the piano, clarinet and violin at St Marylebone, which was also the only school in the London area with its own rabbi and which held separate Christian and Jewish morning assemblies.

Dr Terence Kingston Derry, a brilliant history teacher, has remained a lifelong inspiration. He treated us as though we were taking part in a university tutorial. He made us think and expected us to read widely. He was married to a Norwegian princess and had been involved throughout the Second World with the so-called 'Shetland Bus', the nickname of a clandestine special operations group that made a permanent link between Shetland, Scotland, and German-occupied Norway from 1941 until the German occupation ended on 8 May 1945. The Shetland Bus was operated by an incredibly brave bunch of Norwegian fishermen using tiny fishing boats with small single cylinder diesel engines, operating perforce in the worst winter weather and at night because those elements gave them natural camouflage. The group's main purpose was to transfer agents in and out of Norway, and supply them with weapons, radios and other equipment. They were involved in secret military operations inside Norway and also brought out Norwegians who feared arrest by the Germans. Dr Derry, known simply as T.K., had written a book about the military campaign in Norway and was a visiting professor of history at Cornell University in New York. In summer he ran school camps in East Sussex and organised walking expeditions. I crossed the Brecon Beacons on one of his trips, staying in youth hostels. He roused in me a serious love of outdoor activities, inspiring me to campaign in Parliament to this day for outdoor education.

At that time I was 'Navy mad'. I was determined to win a scholarship to the Royal Naval College at Dartmouth in Devon so that I could have a career at sea. Outside school I was pursuing a 'virtual' career in the London Sea Cadet Corps, taking every possible course, with Dartmouth very much in mind. I rowed in 10-oared whaling boats on the Thames and sailed dinghies around Eel Pie Island, the only inhabited island in the lower Thames and famous for its eel pies, loved by King Henry VIII, and raucous rock concerts in the 1960s featuring such groups as The Rolling Stones and The Who.

After qualifying as a sea cadet petty officer, I was attached in 1956 to HMS *Plover*, a car ferry converted to a mine layer, taking part in a huge NATO exercise in the Baltic Sea. Other cadets and I slept on the mine deck in hammocks that swayed about among the practice mines. In Copenhagen I went ashore and spent a wonderful afternoon in the Tivoli Gardens listening to a free Mozart and Tchaikovsky concert given by the Danish State Radio Orchestra. I walked back to the ship and turned in early. The next morning it was fascinating to watch the Navy ratings trying to take care of their own as they returned from shore leave. One of the matelots had got back at about 7am absolutely stotious drunk and his mates were trying to get him into his uniform so he could at least appear on parade. They managed to get him into his Number Eights, the working kit of dark blue trousers and light blue shirt, but the poor fellow fell over despite their efforts to hold him upright for inspection and he had to spend a night in the cell.

This enthusiasm for the Royal Navy might seem militaristic, especially given my later long involvement with CND, but I was highly motivated by the idea of serving my country. For years after the end of the Second World War all the boys' comic books and much other reading targeted at schoolboys featured deeds of action and 'glory'. It was in effect a not too subtle extension of the anti-German and anti-Japanese propaganda that was understandably and deliberately put out during the war. Regrettably, for decades after the conflict ended and the founders of the European Union had provided a new vision of how peoples can live in peace, Germans continued to be caricatured either as 'evil Huns' or occasionally as honourable but ruthless warriors. I am so glad that I have now many much-loved German and Austrian friends.

As soon as I turned 16 I made my application to Dartmouth. That year there were more than 300 applicants for just ten places. There were a range of academic, intellectual aptitude, medical and physical fitness tests.

I sat the first written exam in a room somewhere in Whitehall. Most of it was to do with mental and observational logic. I passed that and travelled the 160 miles to Dartmouth for a three-day residential in which the finalists sat more exams and were given problem-solving challenges in teams. I was in a group that passed everything. I was summoned again to Whitehall for a medical but failed my eye test. I was devastated. There was nothing else I wanted to do. With hindsight, I am not sure that a life in the Navy would have suited me and I would not swap the life I subsequently led.

Meanwhile, I passed eight 'O' levels while Dad was posted to HMS *Fulmar*, the Royal Navy Fleet Air Arm station near the fishing port of Lossiemouth on Scotland's Moray Firth. The Air Arm operated combat, support and training aircraft out of *Fulmar* and there were constant landings and take-offs by U.S. and Canadian Air force planes on NATO patrol duties. The airfield had been built to combat the German threat during the Second World War, but paradoxically in 1958 while we lived there the first German Naval Air Squadron to be trained in Britain was posted to *Fulmar* and the pilots of both sides formed lifelong friendships. Pilot officers of the Indian Navy's 300 Squadron also arrived for training. In the early 1970s the Royal Navy handed Lossiemouth to the RAF as its main British base for state-of-the-art 1,300 miles per hour Tornado and Lightning stealth multirole fighter aircraft.

There was much family discussion after I passed my 'O' levels as to whether I should go as a boarder to my father's old school, Bedford, to study until 'A' level. I felt viscerally rebellious about the idea of going to a 'posh' public school. I insisted on staying with the family and we all moved 600 miles north to Lossiemouth and into officers' married quarters on the fringe of the town.

I now went to Elgin Academy, one of the oldest schools in Scotland, dating back to the Middle Ages. I played rugby there for one season, but we won only one match – against nearby Gordonstoun private school where the heir to the British throne, Prince Charles, was a pupil. The teaching at Elgin was rigorous and I passed English and History at Higher level, roughly the equivalent of the English 'A' level, and French at Lower level, the equivalent of the English 'O' level.

It was while living at Lossiemouth that my brother Euan developed a love for the air, and he went on to enjoy a long career as a commercial airline pilot. But at this time Euan was a very keen birdwatcher and I loved walking with him along the cliffs that stretched eastwards beyond Lossiemouth's long flat beach of golden sand backed by dunes.

If we were lucky we spotted grey seals offshore and sometimes bottle-nosed dolphins leaping from the water as they came very close to shore to catch salmon gathering to enter the mouths of the Rivers Spey, Lossie and Findhorn. The most remarkable birds were the fulmars, after which the naval air station was named. They nest on cliffs and even in some cases are known to dig holes in the sides of dunes where there is enough grass to support a roof and make their nests. They would glide with incredible speed and precision just above the windblown grass and heather and sometimes whizzed past us just a couple of feet away at knee height. Their stiff winged flight was quite extraordinary to watch.

Euan once found a huge black-backed gull that was not very well and we carried it back to the house and put it on the table on some newspapers in our little upstairs rumpus room. It was as big as the biggest turkey and very intimidating. It just sat staring at us with a glaucous eye and silently died after three days. Mum was not impressed as she had just read an article in the Aberdeen *Press and Journal* about a wee boy who had lost his finger to just such a seabird. I am surprised Euan bothered. I remember once he found a pigeon at the foot of the church tower at St Marks Church in London. It was so badly damaged that it was clear that the kindest thing to do was to put it out of its misery. Euan closed his eyes and wrung its neck. Horrifically, its head came right off with its little red eyes still blinking at us.

While we lived in Lossiemouth, I went on the Moray Sea School course run by Outward Bound at nearby Burghead. Outward Bound was founded in 1941 to give young men the confidence to survive if their ships went down in the North Atlantic. The model was so successful that when the war was over young men and women from all walks of life were sent on courses with remarkable results. Burghead was the first Outward Bound school in Scotland, and the experience built on those under T.K. Derry in reinforcing my opinion that outdoor learning had to be central to any good education system.

We were a motley bunch at Burghead. Some had been sent as part of their job training from Glasgow by employers who ranked abilities such as empathy, ability to judge, ability to get on with others, overall self-confidence and initiative as equal to passing exams in the basic skills of maths and English. In Norway they recognise the importance of learning outside the classroom to the extent that in primary schools by law all children must spend at least one day a week outside the classroom. I would like to see something equivalent applied in Scotland and Britain more widely.

10

An organic princely paradise

They were the richest clover meadows I had ever seen. It was an organic paradise, free of synthetic pesticides, chemical fertilisers, genetically modified organisms and controversial animal feed additives.

As cows grazed on big organic red and white clover flowers, fat Tamworth pigs, one of Britain's oldest breeds, roamed a nearby field and wallowed contentedly in mud baths. Magnificent hedges and trees lined pastures, the wild flower meadows and oat and wheat fields renewed by old-fashioned crop rotation and manured with natural compost instead of nitrogen-based fertilisers made from fossil fuels.

Beyond the main house, leading to the 1,100-acre organic farm, stretched reed beds absorbing domestic and farm waste water and effluents, filtering out contaminants and returning pure water to the farm streams and ponds.

It was October 2000, just a year after I had made the Green breakthrough into a UK legislature. I was at the Duchy Home Farm of Prince Charles, heir to the British throne, at Highgrove in Gloucester shire to witness what could be achieved by dedicated organic farming because I had been given a historic opportunity by Scotland's new Parliament to introduce organic farming legislation. I wanted to gather a few ideas from Home Farm, which Prince Charles decided in 1986 to convert to a completely organic system.

Under the Scottish Parliament's innovative modern system, every elected representative gets one chance in each Parliament's four-year life to introduce a private member's bill. I was torn between legislating on organic farming or introducing a bill on promoting house insulation which, in a cool country like ours, can save huge sums of money on fuel consumption and expenditure.

I decided in the end to introduce an Organic Food and Farming Targets Bill, to give it its full solemn title. It set a target of 20 per cent of our farmland being farmed organically and healthily by 2012. Arguing the case, I said there was not enough government support and advice to help farmers convert to organics. I argued also that organic food was increasingly sought by consumers but that 75 percent of organic food on sale came from outside Britain: this needed to change.

My first task was to recruit the minimum 11 MSP signatures necessary for the bill to be debated. My fellow non-mainline Musketeers, Denis Canavan and Tommy Sheridan, signed up. My philosophy of engaging constructively with parliamentarians of all parties paid off when I got signatures also from each of the four big parties at Holyrood – Labour, the Scottish Nationalists, the Liberal Democrats and the Conservatives. There was real cross-party enthusiasm for the bill and all the signatories, more than 40 of them in the 129-member assembly, saw it as a fine chance for our young Parliament to have a positive and real impact on Scotland.

We made five main arguments for the Organic Bill.

First, organic food was great for you. It delivered the highest-quality, best-tasting food, produced without chemical fertilisers or poisonous pest controls. Just try this test some time: buy a factory-produced chicken from a supermarket chain and a plump free-range chicken from an organic farm and taste the huge difference. The free-range chicken, which lives happier, is infinitely more delicious. Really! A four-year £12m European Union-funded investigation into the difference between organic and ordinary farming has shown that organic foods have far more nutritional value. Up to 40 per cent more antioxidants, which scientists believe can cut the risk of heart disease and cancer, are found in organic fruit and vegetables than in those conventionally farmed.[1]

Second, animal welfare is at the heart of organic systems. Organic standards protect all aspects of animal well-being – from rearing, feeding and shelter to transport and shelter. Compare Prince Charles'

[1] 'Organic food is healthier and safer, four-year EU investigation shows,' by Emily Dugan in *The Independent*, 29 October 2007.

Tamworth pigs wallowing happily in their royal mud with the nightmare of factory sows, tethered with their snouts literally in feeding troughs in darkness and unable to turn and nurture their piglets sucking on their teats. The latter bears comparison to the worst kind of concentration camp.

Third, genetically modified (GM) crops are banned under organic standards. Greens and many scientists argue that the potential risks to human health of interfering in nature with GM seeds and crops are simply not known, and therefore are risks not worth taking. More than half a dozen European countries agree with us and have banned GM crops. We argued from 2000 onwards that a GM-free Scotland would promote our international image as a country with pure produce and vast swathes of natural environment. It is intellectually shoddy to claim that science knows and gives thoughtful control over all of the environmental questions which should be asked of GM.[2] The UK government-funded National Environment Research Council (NERC) concluded, in the world's largest environmental impact study of genetically modified crops, that they were bad for wildlife. The report, which monitored 273 experimental fields over six years, said GM sugar beet and oilseed rape supported fewer birds, bees and butterflies than conventional crops.[3] Bayer CropScience, the company that owns the patent on the GM oilseed rape that was tested by the NERC, said after the report's publication that it was not going ahead with its application to grow the crop in Europe. The results were particularly significant because winter-grown oilseed rape occupies 330,000 hectares of British fields – the third-biggest after wheat and barley – and is the crop from which farmers make most money.

Fourth, organic farming encourages wildlife. The technique relies on wildlife to help control natural pests, so wide field margins are left uncultivated for bugs, birds and bees to flourish. These creatures are also not sprayed into oblivion by the chemical fertilisers, chemicals and pesticides routinely used on non-organic farms.

[2] 'Bitter Fruits. The issue of GM crops is too important to leave to science alone.' Brian Wynne, Professor of Science Studies at Lancaster University's Centre for the Study of Environmental Change, the *Guardian*, 17 September 1999.
[3] 'Farm Scale Evaluations.' National Environment Research Council report, 2005.

Fifth, organic farming is clearly best for the health of our fragile planet. More than 20 per cent of Britain's greenhouse carbon dioxide gas emissions come from the farming and food production chain, according to a major British government report. Nitrogen fertiliser manufacture and use is the worst offender: to produce just one tonne of such dressing takes one tonne of petroleum, seven tonnes of greenhouse gases and 100 tonnes of water. 'If greenhouse gases are not reduced, global temperatures could rise by up to 6°C by the end of the century,' said the report. 'This would increase global instability, conflict, public health-related mortality, degradation of natural resources and migrations beyond any of our recent experience.'[4]

Under the rules of the new Parliament I was given a team of civil servants to help with the legal drafting of the bill. Creating legislation is a long, tedious, complex and careful process. Once I had the necessary number of signatures for my initial short proposal, I next had to put it out for consultation. This requires sending a series of questions to as many interested parties as possible. In my case, this involved shops and supermarkets, academic institutions, consumer organisations, nutritionists, the National Farmers Union in Scotland, the Scottish Organic Producers Association and the Soil Association, founded in 1946 by a group of farmers, scientists and nutritionists who observed a direct connection between farming practice and plant, animal, human and environmental health. Today the Soil Association is the UK's leading organic organisation, with more than 200 staff based in Edinburgh and Bristol and working as certification inspectors across the country.

I was helped very much by a small group of farmers and members of the Soil Association, including Hugh Raven, the organisation's director in Scotland, who farms organically and practises wildlife conservation across 60 square miles of Scottish Highland hills, woodland, rivers and lochs.

Next, Parliament's environment committee had to hear evidence and consider the bill. I found my own experience of giving testimony pretty terrifying. I had in front of me a giant folder containing what we hoped were the answers to every possible question. At my elbow was

[4] 'Food 2030.' UK Government report, January 2010.

Mark Ruskell, the Green Party's top expert on organic food and farming.

My suspicions that we would not win in committee were heightened a week before the hearing began when Ross Finnie, the coalition government's rural affairs and environment minister, published a watered down Organic Action Plan, which said subliminally to me, 'This is one half of your bill and it's all you are going to get, chum.' He argued that the government could not accept the bill because it set specific targets, and the government had no such precise control over organic production. It would be wrong, he said, to enforce targets on farmers who were trying to earn a living from market-led demand.[5] Naturally, I spoke out and disagreed. But Finnie did say the government wanted to see Scottish organic food in the marketplace and end a situation in which imported produce met most of Scottish organic food consumer demand. He made a sort of organic oath: 'I believe organic farming has an important contribution to make to the protection and enhancement of our rural environment, and to the provision of good food which customers want.' He pledged that his Action Plan, which Parliament would review once a year, would commit the government to working with organic farmers in an attempt to double the area of good quality farming land in organic production, without setting a specific target date.

It turned out as I feared. The committee voted against and the full chamber of Parliament accepted the committee recommendation and defeated my bill, on which we had laboured for three years. It will be consumer action, public opinion and climate change concerns that drive the organic farming issue back on to the political agenda.

Our hard work has not been entirely in vain. While organic farming has made little discernible progress since the birth of Scotland's Parliament, at least it has not slipped back. And while my bill had not succeeded, I had gathered all-party support and the government had come up with its own organic plan, albeit a far less satisfactory one. A Green issue was on the mainstream agenda. The goal now was to make all Green concerns mainstream.

[5] 'Targets Bill is rejected by MSPs.' *The Scotsman*, 7 February 2003.

11

University years and some near-death experiences

I returned to Marylebone Grammar School for a final year when Pa
was re-posted yet again from Lossiemouth to the Ministry of Defence
in London.

I was picking potatoes in a field near Winchester in a holiday job in
that summer of 1958 when my 'A' level results came through. I had
passed 'A' levels in English, history and French, won the school prizes
for the first two and had only just missed the French prize by a few
marks. To my distress, there was no joy in the Harper household. My
mother said of my results: 'You didn't deserve it. You didn't work
hard enough.'

This triggered tensions that took years to dispel. I had become
increasingly critical of what I conceived to be my parents' snobbery.
Mixing with the Navy's officer class, Mum had become very conscious
of social demands in terms of orderly behaviour and simply wanted
Euan and me to conform. I am afraid that I found it all very restrictive.
Both, and in particular my mother, were very conscious of their social
class and standing and loved having high-ranking friends. When I
lapsed into a London working-class Cockney accent, Mum would say:
'You're beginning to sound like an oik.' [An oik is described in the
Collins English dictionary as someone who behaves 'in a rude or
unacceptable way, especially in a way that you believe to be typical of
a low social class'!] Two of my closest friends spoke with wonderfully
colourful and expressive Cockney accents, and I felt it very unfair that
they should be typecast because of the way they spoke the English
language. After all, one of the glories of Britain is its wealth of very
different regional accents.

My folks wanted me to go to Oxford or Cambridge. But my inverted snobbery gene kicked in and I said I wanted to go to one of the new English universities that were then being opened, upon which my parents said there was no way they would agree to pay for me to go to a redbrick university. If I would not consider Oxford or Cambridge, they said, I would have to go to one of Scotland's four ancient universities.

I applied to study history – against the advice of the school, which urged me to take English – at Edinburgh, Aberdeen, St Andrews and Glasgow. All except Aberdeen required 'O' level Latin, which I had not taken, as part of their entrance requirements. Aberdeen accepted me, and in October 1958 I boarded a steam train at London's King's Cross station, accompanied by a huge brassbound trunk and a small suitcase, for what was then a long overnight journey hundreds of miles northwards to the city on the North Sea coast and its five-centuries-old university.

Pa gave me an allowance of £10 a week to cover all my living expenses, including academic books. This was generous because four years later that was all I earned as a salary in Glasgow teaching at Crookston Castle School. Initially I took digs in south Aberdeen, with my landlady providing breakfast and dinner.

As a first year undergraduate – called a *bajan*, from the French 'béjaune', meaning young bird, or 'bec jaune' (yellow beak) – I wore a truncated red gown with a purple collar. Aberdeen University students lost for ever a two foot-length of their once flowing robes in the 1500s when they mock-trialled an unpopular church sacrist, charged with the care of a church and its contents, and mock-sentenced him to death. When they put a sack over his head and marched him towards an imaginary scaffold, the poor fellow collapsed and died of a heart attack. The entire student population of the day was punished in this way because Aberdeen's winter is long and cold, and the loss of a length of the warm gown, which now came only down to the knees, was a chastening penalty.

I was advised, as the term began, to double up my four-year history honours degree studies with English. I ignored the guidance, adding to the ever-growing pile of advice I had rejected, often to my own

67

detriment. I enjoyed the British history courses with Professor John Hargreaves in my first and second years, but as part of the general introduction to the degree in the first year I failed moral philosophy and French examinations. I passed moral philosophy when I resat the exam in September, but failed French again: unless I passed it eventually, I would not be awarded a degree.

In my second year I shared a flat with a young assistant history lecturer, Arthur Marwick, an extravagant personality and outstanding teacher who went on to become the first Professor of History at Britain's Open University, the innovative distance-learning higher education institution founded in 1969 and funded by the UK Government. The Open University required no entry qualifications other than a clear ability from life experience to study, and it has become the largest academic institution in Europe by student numbers.

Marwick was a wild drinker and womaniser – he officially listed his interests as 'wine, women and football' – with trenchant opinions. From an intellectually austere Quaker family background, he taught a second-year course on the history of labour and socialist movements which I found outstanding. Although his politics were left-wing, he was critical of Marxism. He was contemptuous of the pretensions of fashionable 'postmodernist' critical theories, seeing them as a 'menace to serious historical study'. He became one of Britain's most outstanding and flamboyant social historians and wrote many books, one of them a lucidly written classic, *The Deluge*, a brilliant study of the impact of the First World War on British society published in 1965. Alternatively wonderful, outrageous and dangerous to know, his career might not have flourished in today's cautious and correct academia. I owe to him an introduction to James Maxton – the Scottish socialist politician who derived his convictions from the grinding poverty of many of the children he taught while a schoolteacher in Glasgow – and to Italian opera, which Marwick adored. I would occasionally sit weeping at the records he played in the flat.

In that second year I threw myself into everything that university had to offer – sport, especially running, debating, learning to play the guitar and writing for the university student newspaper *Gaudie*. Nevertheless, I grew bored. Not with my social activities nor with

Marwick's and Hargreaves' social and economic history courses, but with mediaeval history which, paradoxically, I now read with great interest. It is difficult to describe my feelings at the time, since I was still very young. But I came to understand that I was suffering from depression, a serious illness which was not then well understood. We now know that it is quite common, and that about 15 per cent of people will have a bout of severe depression at some point in their lives. At the university medical practice, I was prescribed purple hearts as an anti-depressant. These were also one of the early recreational drugs, 'uppers', a combination of amphetamine and barbiturate, coloured purple and heart-shaped, giving a wide-awake buzz and increased confidence and energy. I took one and the effect was terrifying. I felt ridiculously high, light-headed and deliriously happy and did not like it. I feared addiction, so I chucked the tablets, then being sold on Britain's streets by pushers to kids at anything between one-shilling-and-sixpence and two-shillings-and-sixpence (7p and 12p) a tablet, or £1 for 40. I threw away all the purple hearts and did my best to address my depression in other ways, including getting incredibly fit by cross-country running and competing in middle-distance athletics track events. I have continued to suffer bouts of depression and, in my later professional roles, have taken a special interest in the effects of depression on youngsters for whom I have had some responsibility.

It had been easy to do well at grammar school, but university was much more competitive, and there were a lot of people who had done their military National Service and who had learned how to work hard and to play hard. I became increasingly demotivated and decided I wanted to quit and DO something in the outside world and maybe return to university when I was better prepared for it.

Returning home at the end of the summer term in 1960, I told my parents I could not face another two university years completing an honours degree. My greatest wish was to get out into the real world and do something active that I considered worthwhile. To that end, I told them, I had already secured a job as a draughtsman in a north London architects' office.

My parents were extremely disturbed, and my father, disapproving of the lifestyle in the flat I shared with Marwick and others, had already visited Aberdeen and decided that as a condition of his continuing to support my studies I would have to enter Crombie Hall, an official university residence in the heart of Old Aberdeen and close to most of the academic departments. In fact, life in the flat had not been much different from that of other students' flat lives – gloriously disorganised; parties every other weekend; little pots of porridge kept in drawers that I ate cold, heated up or even fried.

Truth be told, those eating habits caused problems about which I never told my parents. In those first two years I had also played rugby occasionally for the university third fifteen, was elected president of the tiddlywinks club and became for a short while secretary of the Liberal Association. It was while showering one day after a training run that I saw a pool of blood at my feet. The blood was gushing from my mouth. I fled to the university doctor, an elderly man who had been on Captain Robert Falcon Scott's ill-fated expedition to the Antarctic, who told me I was suffering from vitamin C deficiency, or scurvy, and that he had not seen an adult example of it for decades. He said I was bleeding from my gums and mucous membranes. He prescribed an immediate course of vitamin C and other vitamins, and told me I must modify my vitamin C-deficient diet of porridge, fish and chips and copious beer.

The doctor recalled that Scott's expeditions had suffered from scurvy which had been put down to tainted meat. It was only in 1932 that the connection between vitamin C and scurvy was established by an American researcher, Charles Glen King, at the University of Pittsburgh. Historically, scurvy was most prevalent among sailors, infants and the elderly, and the legend grew, and continues to this day, that I was the last known adult Scot in history to suffer from the ailment.

At home in London in July 1960 I faced a kind of family tribunal in which I was the accused and faced a formidable prosecution line-up, led by my parents, my father's eldest brother, Lt-Col Ralph Harper OBE, and Pa's second eldest brother, Bob, recently retired as Malaya's Police Commissioner. The case against me was that, although I received a grant from the London County Council for my fees, Pa had paid out of his own pocket for two years for my subsistence. I therefore had a moral duty to give him a return on his investment, not least because no other Harper had ever attended university, and should return to Aberdeen forthwith.

I dug my heels in and said I would only go back if I was allowed to abandon honours studies and complete an ordinary three-year degree which, in normal circumstances, should have taken just one more year of my time. This compromise was agreed, and I travelled to Aberdeen in a deep depression, partly because philosophy and logic courses in my first two years had made me begin to question some of my basic and strong Christian beliefs.

I picked myself up, chose zoology and botany courses and continued with French, which I failed yet again, resulting in having to return for a fourth year to complete my ordinary degree. After yet one more French resit I finally graduated in October 1962. No family member attended my graduation ceremony, but when I ascended the stage to collect my degree there were huge cheers from my many friends and supporters. After this I set off for Glasgow, Crookston Castle and a whole new life with Bennett, Lachlan, Monahan and others.

* * *

My brush with scurvy apart, I experienced a near-death disaster from my drinking habits. I am described nowadays by old friends as having been rather wild and excitable, and after imbibing relatively small amounts of alcohol was prone to climbing walls, buildings, lampposts and anything that was high. There were a number of times I could have fallen and died. Nowadays, although I no longer recognise this young man and am mildly ashamed of him, I still break out occasionally in cold sweats and shivers go down my spine at the memory of the foot that could have slipped or the drainpipe that could have come away from the wall as I climbed back into Crombie Hall past curfew. On visits to Aberdeen I still see the strategic strip of copper beneath a window that was one of my important hand holds. I recall one evening when I drunkenly tried to tiptoe along a wall that had a huge drop beneath it. I am actually seriously scared of heights but I was so drunk that I did not notice the drop. A slip and a fall would have resulted in certain death. There were many crazy stunts by other students. I know of one youth who was intercepted by police while running down the city's main street in the depths of winter stark naked, but for a single sock – and that was not on either of his feet!

There was also an occasion when I agreed to be barman at a formal university party and students gave me a bottle of what was described as 'blackcurrant wine' for my personal consumption. On return to my bedroom my limbs went completely rigid. It emerged that the drink consisted of Ribena blackcurrant concentrate to disguise the fact that it was heavily laced with pure ethyl alcohol. I was diagnosed as suffering from severe alcohol poisoning and told that I could easily have drunk enough to kill me if the party had not finished before the bottle was drained.

Alcohol is Scotland's nationally accepted drug, playing its part in everything from church communions to funerals and ship launches. In the Scots language we probably have more words for inebriation than Eskimos have for snow.

Some four decades later, when I became the highly respectable Rector of Edinburgh University, my former drinking experiences enabled me to take an informed stand against the promotion by clubs and pubs of binge drinking among undergraduates. I warned that accidents were waiting to happen and it would be no surprise if there were deaths among university students from alcohol poisoning. I have consistently urged government authorities to curb cheap drink offers. The real price of alcoholic drinks is now about one-third what it was in the 1960s. There is a real connection between the cost of alcohol and the amount people drink, and the statistics show we now consume two to three times more alcohol than we did in the 1960s. I still enjoy a drink, but support absolutely any move, including raising the price of alcoholic drinks, that would reduce the damage that has been done to our society and people's health by excessive drinking.

12

Fruits of the struggle

The second general election to the Scottish Parliament was held on 1 May 2003. I was aged 62 and, as the only Green Party MSP throughout the Parliament's first four years of life, I had had to learn how to survive a punishing schedule, addressing hundreds of meetings and press conferences and appearing almost non-stop on television and radio while writing columns for newspapers.

We now needed to make a major advance by persuading voters to elect more Greens and move the party into a higher league.

We had made sufficient impact for the Green Party to have three times as many supporters campaigning for us nationally than in 1999. Four years earlier I had concentrated all my efforts in Edinburgh and the Lothians. This time I campaigned throughout the country. All the past hard work meant I was recognised wherever I went. Little old ladies waved umbrellas and handbags at me, saying such things as 'I know you. You're the Green Man!' They may not have known my name, but my face, my rainbow Dr Who scarf and the idea of Green all gelled together.

With our giant green '2' from 1999 enjoying retirement as a historic treasure in the vaults of the National Museum for Scotland, we needed a replacement. I commissioned the same designer, Martin Budd, to rattle off seven copies of a more manoeuverable and easily stowed Green '2' in polystyrene, one for each of the country's seven 'list' constituencies. Held aloft, the '2s' looked great when our top candidates in each of the national constituencies assembled for our manifesto launch on the steps of Dynamic Earth, a modern science centre next to the Scottish Parliament.

The Green Party has always tried to campaign in innovative and cheerful ways. I have a particularly huge concern for the marine environment, and in 2003 the Whale and Dolphin Society loaned us Lucy, a 10 metre-long inflatable Orca killer whale, to illustrate one of our campaign pledges – to protect whales and dolphins around Scotland's coastline. We took her to Leith Docks, Edinburgh's port, in the pouring rain: she glistened as though she had just leapt out of the ocean. I was photographed kissing her nose, not recommended with the real thing as Orcas have big teeth. We carried this campaign forward into the third Parliament when in 2010 I introduced an amendment to the government's Marine Bill to declare Scotland's entire coastal seas a whale and dolphin sanctuary. We deliberately left out any scales of punishment, other than to say it would be illegal to harass or kill cetaceans off Scotland. We were told – although we already knew – that the spirit of our amendment was embodied in several international agreements that the UK government had signed. This was not the point, I argued. Given threats by countries such as Japan, Iceland and Norway to resume commercial whaling, and the unashamed bribery by Japan of small developing countries to deliver pro-whaling votes on the International Whaling Commission, set up in 1946 to conserve stocks and regulate commercial whaling, Scotland's Parliament needed to make its own bold public statement. We needed to say loudly that there were so few whales left in North Atlantic waters that we at least would not be killing any – unlike Norway, for example, which kills about a thousand Minke whales each year – and that naming Scotland's seas as a sanctuary would send a positive and morally justified message far beyond our boundaries.

The amendment was defeated, sadly. Its impact, if carried, would have been fantastic for Scotland and for Britain more generally. Parliament really missed a trick here: it would have given a huge boost to the tourist industry and to our existing small-scale whale- and dolphin-watching enterprises in the Moray Firth and off the west coast. It will be no surprise if one day a ruling party or coalition reactivates our proposal as their own and makes it law.

* * *

We knew that once again in 2003 we had to get out the second vote in the proportional representation section of the election to ensure we increased our numbers in Parliament. We printed 'Second Vote Green' posters and handed out little green windmills across the country to passers-by to illustrate what we were all about.

We had jammed ajar the door of the Scottish Parliament in 1999. Now we sought to push it wide open. Part of our strategy was to inspire pride among our fellow Scots in their innovative Parliament, which one distinguished commentator said was already making Westminster look like a museum, 'a quaint Victorian establishment where tourists can go to see how politics used to be in the old days and laugh at the funny men in tights.'[1]

We argued that the presence of a dissenting, but constructive, minority voice like the Green Party's in Parliament would make a real difference to the way politics was conducted and to citizens' lives. Tony Blair's Labour Party had won landslide majorities in the 1997 and 2001 Westminster general elections, but the Blair government proved relentlessly, by its conduct, that an administration elected purely on a first-past-the-post system could ignore large and important minorities, governing by nod and wink, with backbench MPs facing near-impossible tasks when it came to influencing government decisions or limiting the power of the ruling party machine. The 59 per cent turnout in the 2001 Westminster election was the poorest voting performance for a century: 17,000,000 people, nearly half the electorate, had not bothered to vote. And of the votes that *were* cast, Labour secured only 42 per cent while winning 60 per cent of the seats! Here was a stark democratic deficit. 'Few if any [Westminster] MPs are seen as speaking fearlessly for their people,' lamented Hugo Young, the *Guardian*'s chief political commentator. 'If collections of them [MPs] purport to do so, they're cast into the salon of those self-excluded from serious society.' Young, who in the final years of his life (he died in late 2003) became ever-more despairing about the health of British democracy, warned that Labour ministers were deepening the alienation of ordinary voters from the system in which Westminster politicians worked. 'Voters are better educated,' he said. 'They're harder to fob off with fancy claims. They're less deferential to leaders

[1] Iain Macwhirter, *Sunday Herald*, 27 May 2001

of all kinds, less willing to believe in anyone or anything, less chained by prior ideological allegiance.'[2]

Young's thinking mirrored my own and that of most Green Party supporters. Scots had created something entirely new and healthy within British democracy. The House of Commons at Westminster was designed for confrontation in bygone centuries, with the front benches exactly three sword lengths apart just in case the leader of the opposition ever decided to disembowel the prime minister. The Scottish Parliament's shape, a less confrontational semi-circle, lessens the temptation to indulge in contrived wars of words at the expense of serious debate. Instead of queuing to troop through mediaeval-era wood-panelled voting lobbies, as at Westminster, each MSP has a small desk console with three buttons – NO, ABSTAIN and YES. Each vote takes only 30 seconds and voting takes place only at 5pm, so no one needs to be hauled from offices, meetings, beds, bars and restaurants by division bells to vote at any time of the day or night, as at Westminster. It is how most sensible modern democracies conduct their business, and I am certain there are many Westminster MPs who wish they could adopt our efficient system for themselves.

Scotland's two-vote arrangement has produced not landslide majorities but coalition governments in which all shades of opinion have had to be considered. Power-sharing in Scotland pre-dated by more than a decade the situation in which, by an accident of the first-past-the-post system, Conservatives and Liberal Democrats found themselves having to share power at Westminster from 2010 onwards.

With Scotland's Parliament shaping its own very different approach to affairs, light years different from Westminster, decisions on key areas of Scottish life – health, education, justice and more – were now being taken in Edinburgh instead of 500 miles away in London. Environmental issues grew steadily in importance, and by the time we began campaigning for the 2003 election I was measuring our success not only by how well the Green Party seemed to be doing but by the extent to which the big traditional parties were falling over themselves

---

[2] Hugo Young, 'Message of the polls: the age of froth is over,' the *Guardian*, 19 September 2000.

to cherry-pick our agenda to prove which of them was the fairest Green of all. It was a fundamental Green dilemma, both for us in Scotland and for fellow Greens on mainland Europe, that the better we performed the more others would take on environmental issues and try to squeeze us out. It was not a problem that bothered me as long as environmental and climate change issues moved ever higher up the overall political agenda.

Once the 2003 votes had been counted, it turned out that we were surfing a remarkable Green wave. I was joined in the second Scottish Parliament by six additional Green Party MSPs. We had sprung the trap of just being the cuddly Robin Harper Green Party and had been fully recognised by voters as serious players in Scotland's political game.

The scenes in the Edinburgh and Lothians count at Meadowbank Stadium were extraordinary as the news trickled through from the rest of Scotland, via people's cellphones, in the early morning that Greens and Socialists were winning seats everywhere. We all became very excited and when Colin Fox, the Socialist candidate for Lothian, heard he had been elected he completely lost control and ran round and round the huge hall whooping with delight. The Green Party had not been confident of getting two candidates elected on the Edinburgh and Lothians list, but when Mark Ballard learned he had been elected as the constituency's second Green he climbed on a counting table and began dancing, and I joined him.

Shortly after the election, we arranged a national Green Party council meeting in a room above the Bell Inn in Edinburgh's Grass-market to discuss the way forward. It proved to be the toughest get-together that I have ever attended before or since with senior party members. During the first Parliament, I had been the *de facto* leader of the party as the lone elected Green. Beyond the legislature, however, our party structure was far more complicated. Stay with me here . . .

Both the Scottish Green Party and the English and Welsh Green Party memberships were opposed to hierarchies and having a tradi-tional 'leader'. However, under election law, all competing parties were required by the Electoral Commission to nominate a leader. So, solely for the purpose of the contest, the party gave the title of nominal leader to one of our candidates, Dr Eleanor Scott, a Gaelic-speaking paediatrician from the Scottish Highlands.

With seven Green Party MSPs newly elected, the 'leader'/'co-convenors' problem had to be tackled at the Bell Inn council meeting. Given that the majority of delegates wanted co-convenors, which I disagreed with, I felt it was probably the right time to announce that I was ready to pass on the baton of leadership gracefully while serving out my own second four-year term as a Green Party parliamentarian. I felt it might be wise also to make way for new talent to come through in my own Edinburgh and Lothians constituency: with two elected Green MSPs, the constituency could be regarded now as the party's only fairly safe seat.

Shiona Baird MSP, a farmer from near Dundee, became the Green Party's female 'co-convenor'. I was alongside her as male 'co-convenor'. No progress was made at the Bell Inn meeting towards establishing when the party might at some point seriously consider electing a clear leader, and for the four-year life of that second Scottish Parliament the question was not raised again. I have always believed there are times to keep one's own counsel and simply wait to see how events unfold, and that is what I now did in the wake of the leadership controversy.

Shiona Baird and I managed to work out a sharing of responsibilities, deciding, for example, to take it in turns to raise issues at First Minister's[3] question time on behalf of the party, although I have to admit I was never at ease with the format. My natural instinct is dialogue rather than diatribe and I hated the preparatory sessions with team members who wanted me to work myself up into some kind of phoney angry lather concerning issues I wanted to deal with calmly and rationally and with dignity.

Shiona, in contrast, seemed quite at ease in her role. She managed to assume an admonitory grandmotherly stance, gently sandbagging the government whenever she took her turn. She was a good performer.

I feel very strongly that after I step down from Parliament the Green

---

[3] The leader of Scotland's government is not known by the more widely used title of Prime Minister, but as the First Minister.

Party will have to address the problem of leadership with great seriousness before our cause can advance. The England and Wales Green Party decided that its ideological stance of having no single leader was counter-productive. Abandoning the dogma, it elected in 2008 a Leader and Deputy Leader and less than two years later Caroline Lucas was elected the first Westminster Green Party MP in the May 2010 British general election.

Our party members will have to come to understand that it is essential for the Scottish Green Party, like other parties, to have an official Leader and face to represent it if it is to sustain political effectiveness. Eventually we will have to follow the path our England and Wales brothers and sisters have taken – preferably sooner rather than later. A Leader does not need to be given huge individual powers, only a huge amount of internal support to enable him or her to relate effectively with the media and to promote to the widest possible audience the party's policies and ideals.

13

An unconventional interview opens up a career with an education guru

I completed my Diploma of Education in 1964 at Aberdeen College of Education. I was lucky. Somehow I managed to arrive a day late for the final examination paper, but the College's excellent history lecturer, George Grieve, did me a huge favour, ushered me into a room to write the exam and I became a fully qualified schoolteacher.

I returned home for the summer to London where Pa, on retiring from the Navy, had become secretary of the Flying Angel Mission, an international Christian organisation providing support and shelter to sailors in more than 230 ports around the world.

Pa and Mum moved into a flat that came with the job in Ecclestone Square, next door to the residence of the Papal legate (ambassador) to the United Kingdom. Whenever Archbishop Igino Eugenio Cardinale received a call from Pope Paul VI in Rome we could hear the phone ring next door.

I had taken a temporary job checking examination paper results for City and Guilds, an industrial skills academic organisation, but I had already decided I wanted to teach in Scotland. George Grieve, whose teaching methods along with his forgiving nature had had a profound effect on me, rang to say the trailblazing educationist R.F. Mackenzie was about to pass through London, after a holiday in France, and was seeking progressive teachers for his extraordinarily innovative Braehead Secondary School in the small Scottish coal mining town of Buckhaven on the Fife coast. I had been deeply inspired by a lecture Mackenzie had given at the College of Education, and Grieve wanted to make sure I grabbed the chance to get together with Mackenzie.

We arranged to meet at The Cambridge, a famous pub in Charing

Cross Road near Cambridge Circus, the fictional headquarters of MI6 in John le Carré's George Smiley spy novels.

I had just won £15 on the horses with a half-crown (12p!) double, so I was in a mood to celebrate and down some ale. Mackenzie also liked his beer. We talked and talked and talked for some four hours and drank a few pints. I spoke about my teaching experiences in Glasgow and of changes I would like to see made in the Scottish education system. Mackenzie, one of the most original and controversial thinkers about education in 20th-century Britain, talked about how his ideas developed while teaching in the mid-1930s at the Forest School, in Hampshire's New Forest. The school had been established by a radical Quaker to provide an imaginative education, much of it outdoors, for working-class children. Later, in 1938, Mackenzie was living with a Jewish family in Germany when their house was attacked by Nazi Brownshirts. Returning to Britain, he joined the Royal Air Force and served as a navigator aboard Lancaster bombers.

By 10pm we were both feeling quite light-headed. Mackenzie needed to get back to his family, who were staying in Dulwich in the south of London, so I walked him towards Charing Cross to catch the tube train. Just as I was saying farewell, I realised he had not said a word about whether or not he was offering me a job. I jogged his memory about the main purpose of our meeting and he replied with a huge smile: 'Of course you've got the job.' We shook hands on my appointment to my first full-time post as a professionally qualified teacher. I virtually skipped home through the streets of London to give the news to my parents who, for once, were quite pleased with what I had achieved.

I packed my bag and travelled north to four years of deeply satisfying but extremely demanding work. Right from the start, in 1957, of Mackenzie's reign at Braehead it had become an extraordinary and important school. While a new comprehensive school was being built, which would eventually take in all the children of the area, Mackenzie was asked to teach the 'has-beens and the ranks of the never were', 11-plus rejects in what was then called a junior secondary school (the equivalent of the first three years of a modern secondary school in England). The kids were seen as predestined failures, doomed to achieve nothing academically, to pass no exams and to have limited chances of employment in those tough times in East Fife. Many of the kids could have been the brothers and sisters of my old pal Bennett at Crookston Castle School in Glasgow. Buckhaven and nearby Methil had one of the highest unemployment rates in Scotland: one area of Methil was so tough that it was known locally as Dodge City.

Mackenzie, a son of an Aberdeenshire stationmaster, was a charismatic teacher who inspired in his staff the belief that 11-plus rejects were not fated to be failures. He loathed the system that could make heavy judgments on children's future lives at such a young age and told us it was our mission to chart imaginative and successful paths forwards for our children. We should recognise the potential of our pupils, not their deficiencies. We should challenge the received certainties of the then educational establishment and question its truths. We should experiment with democracy and, if necessary, be anarchic, noisy and combative. We should break entirely new ground while being aware that the Establishment would be sniffy and intolerant of anything other than the conventional.

He was as much a social reformer as an educational reformer, a sworn enemy of the Establishment with an absolute belief in the goodness of children. 'The man was difficult, cussed, and at times arrogant. But he had vision, he had compassion in abundance, he had courage, and he had a wonderful, zealous, engaging radicalism that was at times angry, but never truculent,' wrote Harry Reid, editor of the *Glasgow Herald*, in the foreword to a book about Mackenzie.[1] Reid said Mackenzie 'never stopped cajoling us, raising our eyes high to the sky, and teaching, always teaching us, to reject the mendacious and the meretricious, to discard the conventional, to reject the divisive, and – above all – to be kind, and to think well and think big.'

Buckhaven was a run-down old town and the beaches for miles along the coast, which should have been sandy, were covered thickly in black coal waste tipped into the sea by the National Coal Board

---

[1] *The Life of R.F. Mackenzie: A Prophet Without Honour*, by Peter Murphy (published 1998 by John Donald Ltd, Edinburgh).

after the industry was nationalised in 1947. Buckhaven was no longer the stuff of picture postcards, a seaside holiday destination favoured by Glasgow working-class families in the 1920s and 1930s.

I was appointed to teach English, modern studies and history and given huge latitude in how I approached my work. In those days there was no set curriculum for what were dismissively labelled 'non-certificate' pupils. You could construct your own education models, free of the restrictions and pressures of national examination time-tables. As far as I was concerned, everything was possible for the kids in my classes as long as they were given a sense of self-worth and competence.

In practice, we did not give them a watered-down version of the curriculum. I read a translation of Homer's *Iliad* to my classes over several weeks. The rapt attention the 2,500-year-old poem elicited was almost unbelievable. We wrote poetry and discussed Greek culture. I mused how many pupils in Scotland, at any level, had access to the thought, the architectural ideas and political inspiration that came from the ancient Greeks. My own ideas at the time were heavily influenced by the ideas of the Oxford University philosopher R.G. Collingwood, who argued that self-knowledge was as important as historical knowledge and that although it was necessary to establish principles for living one's life it did not mean that some set of unbending rules needed to be slavishly followed.

Rather than make my history classes analyse worthy tomes, I would take pupils down to the coal-covered beaches, where we sat among the waste and pondered how the Neolithic people of Skara Brae on the Orkney Islands used to survive three centuries before Christ. We found clay at the back of the beaches, built cooking pits and heated flat stones on which we fried eggs and boiled water, each step worked out from first principles.

Braehead was distinctive in many ways, but its emphasis on creativity and experience was what stood out most. It had a higher ratio of art and music teachers per pupil than any other school in Scotland – four art teachers and four music teachers for 400 kids.

David Shonfield, with whom I shared a cottage on the slopes of Largo Law, a 1,000 foot-high volcanic hill inland from Buckhaven, taught English and had a classroom at the opposite corner of the school to mine in which he built a theatre stage. His kids learned almost entirely by writing and performing their own plays in two separate quasi-Shakespearean theatre companies, the King's Men and the Globe Company.

Hamish Brown, one of Scotland's most distinguished climbers and adventurers, was appointed to a unique position as the country's first and only full-time outdoor education teacher with a state school. The only times he came into the building were to take the kids away into the hills and countryside, or sometimes to practise rope techniques. A visitor to Braehead might be surprised by seeing boys and girls slithering down ropes from a 30-foot high balcony into the school hall. This was abseiling practice. Originally, Hamish had arrived to teach English but he never got into a classroom: instead he was immediately made responsible by Mackenzie for all expedition activities. Hamish, a member of the Mountain Leadership Training Board, the Scottish Mountaineering Club and the Alpine Club, was given a cottage on Rannoch Moor as a base for expeditions together with a van to transport the kids. He took one bunch of 14- and 15-year-olds and instructed them so well that they all conquered within a 24-hour period the Cuillin Ridge, 22 peaks lying across eight miles of the Isle of Skye, the ascents totalling some 13,000 feet, and one of the most gruelling climbing challenges in Europe. Hamish was especially proud of the fact that the Matterhorn and Jungfrau peaks in the Alps had initials carved on them by his former pupils who ascended the Swiss mountains. Hamish also became my own instructor when I did the Scottish Mountain Leadership course.

Hamish got to know the kids really well on their expeditions. He recalled: 'I had teachers suggesting specific nasty things to do to some of them. But that worked both ways. I once lay in a tent listening to a conversation in the next tent – kids seem to think tents are sound-proof – where they were making up "ropes" of teachers they'd take up Ben Nevis – then cut the rope.'

The technical department was encouraged to build dinghies and kayaks and take the children on waterborne expeditions. Every teacher with an extra skill was encouraged to use it. The head of metalwork took kids gliding. I had my own guitar school. As far as we were concerned there was nothing that was impossible for Braehead's kids. The music department created a rock group and a four-part Bach choir. Paresh Chakraborty, an ever-smiling Brahmin Indian and top-rate painter, taught in the art department as an uncertificated teacher. Although he was better read than most of us and had an excellent command of the English language, he had been unable to get a place at a teacher training college. Nevertheless, he sold his paintings to the British Royal Family's art collection.

One of the art rooms had, for some reason, an enormous coal-fired stove with a great cast-iron kettle constantly on the boil. It became an unofficial staff room where, with classes in progress, other teachers could wander in, make a cup of tea and sit down to watch whatever work was in progress. Pupils wanting to do 'extra art' were also free to enter at any time and work at their easels.

Braehead held a school assembly every day of the week, something few schools do now. Pupils gave readings and presentations, including news of former pupils. Successes were publicly honoured and ap-plauded – and although Mackenzie was opposed to exams our 'failed' kids were passing a spectacular number of 'O' levels. The music each morning included one of the latest pop hits chosen by the pupils' council.

The Braehead School Council had real rather than token powers, again unlike many schools now. It was elected and dealt robustly with bullying, littering, queue-jumping and other offences, as well as organising social events and communicating pupils' concerns direct to Mackenzie. The council even levied small fines – which pupils actually paid. Most school councils in Scotland today are talk shops tightly controlled by a senior teacher, where grievances are aired and very little comes of them. All the kids learn is that democracy does not work.

Paresh, who later became a senior lecturer at an art college in England, and another art teacher, Gordon Campbell, who went on to become a maker of beautiful violins and cellos, ensured that at Christmas the school's walls, on two floors, were decorated by the kids entirely from floor to ceiling with giant murals. Almost everyone, staff and pupils, was involved in music and drama productions to go with whatever the art theme was. The only complaint I recall the school inspectors making was that we had splashed paint on the ceilings! Watching the children create those murals, I had an extraordinary sense of their total absorption and confidence in the creative process. Paint was thrown, brushed and splashed on to huge six-feet-wide rolls of paper to produce stunning results with minimum guidance from staff. Everything we did in the weeks leading to Christmas revolved around the art, music and drama projects. It all resembled a Brazilian carnival – glorious fun, controlled chaos.

Mackenzie was an inspiration to all of us, teachers and children. His ideas were brilliant and he was deeply devoted to the kids and their welfare. But he had his faults, including a spectacularly bad temper, which occasionally erupted like Vesuvius. He was quite clear cut – either you were on his side or you were completely against him. There was no middle ground. Staff meetings could be quite sparky and I tried not to get embroiled in fights with him.

His temper once led him to a temporary abandonment of even his own ideals in a confrontation in relation to the school newspaper, *The Braehead News*. The paper went all over the world. It was edited by the children, who obtained lots of scoops, including an interview with Gerry and the Pacemakers, of 'You'll Never Walk Alone' fame. The girls who did the interview were given sixpenny pieces by Gerry Marsden, the group's leader, which they pierced and wore on silver chains around their necks.

The editors of *The Braehead News* demanded that copy arrive strictly on time. This was necessary because the newspaper was produced on an old-fashioned Gestetner duplicating machine. It was a painful, laborious and messy process, especially as the *News* was produced in colour which meant each page had to be run through the machine up to three times.

On one occasion the machine had already been set up for printing when Mackenzie sent down his own regular column. The pupil editor took the decision to exclude it because Mackenzie had missed the deadline. Mackenzie went bananas, and like some North Korean dictator he closed the newspaper. I had an advisory role to the newspaper team, although I took no part in the editing, and was left speechless when Mackenzie advised me of his decision. I could see it would be useless to argue with him, so I just acknowledged the pronouncement, left his office and went to see the head of English who was volcanically furious, mainly because Mackenzie had betrayed the principles on which the school was being run. He stormed into Mackenzie's office and had a blazing row that could be heard throughout the school. There was a stand-off for several weeks until Bob calmed down and normal service was resumed.

The pupil who refused to publish the headmaster's column became the head of one of Scotland's top radio stations.

14

Jambo,[1] *Mr Harper: The Kenya years*

We learned in 1967 that a decision had been taken to close Braehead School eventually and incorporate it into a new comprehensive school. Mackenzie had been offered a new job at Summerhill Secondary School in Aberdeen. In a sense, Braehead was going to leave me at the end of a very happy and deeply fulfilling few years, and it seemed that fate suggested taking a break to have an adventure.

I had no family responsibilities other than to my parents, who were still comparatively young and in good health, and so I decided to be the master of my fate. I had recently discovered and loved Arthur Grimble's classic book 'A Pattern Of Islands', the true adventures of a British colonial officer in the Pacific Ocean's Gilbert and Ellice Islands. Stranger and funnier than fiction, it was a warm and wonderful story of how Grimble was adopted into the Sun clan, fished for tiger sharks, and grappled – as human bait – with a giant octopus.

I fancied something similar and at much the same time saw a Ministry of Overseas Development advertisement recruiting teachers for posts abroad as part of Britain's commitment to help the progress of developing countries' education systems. I applied and received a letter saying the only posts available were in Kenya and Tanzania, including one where a school was looking for a temporary deputy head teacher.

I was offered, and accepted, the deputy head post at a Kenyan secondary school. I will never forget my last day at Braehead. It was very emotional. I loved the place and the atmosphere. It had become a home to me. Some of the kids I worked with were close to tears. So

---

[1] Jambo is a greeting in Swahili, the main language of East Africa, translating as 'Hello'.

was I. Everyone assembled in the school hall to say farewell. I sang with my pupil folk group and told them all what a lovely lot they were – and indeed they were. I left feeling horribly guilty, not least because Mackenzie had told me he wanted to recommend my promotion to head of the modern studies department if I stayed on until Braehead's final closure.

A few parties later with friends in Fife and Edinburgh, I flew for the first time in a jet plane – a de Havilland Comet, the world's first commercial jet airliner – to London, did a short orientation and introduction course with the Ministry of Overseas Development in Hampshire, and, after a big party at home in Ecclestone Square, went round the corner to the British Overseas Airways Corporation (BOAC) bus station to begin the next chapter of my life.

On arrival in Nairobi, the Kenyan capital, I reported to Jogoo House, headquarters of the national education department. I was told I was being assigned to Kolanya Boys Secondary School in Teso District, some 300 miles to the west of Nairobi near 13,800-foot-high Mount Elgon, famed among naturalists for its elephants and buffaloes which descend deep into caves at night to scrape rock face walls for the salt they contain. When I asked about how to get to Kolanya the official assigned to me told me to return the next day because he and his colleagues had been unable to find it on a map.

When finally they located the place I was given an itinerary involving the hire of several battered Peugeot 404 'taxis' in what looked to be a journey right across Africa. The 404, produced under licence in Kenya, was built like a tank and adapted to carry eight people in great discomfort as a 'bush taxi'. Famously when one of these overcrowded vehicles crashed – as they often did – and all the dead aboard had been counted it was found to have been carrying 16 passengers! Most of the journey was on red laterite roads, known locally as *murram* roads, that were rutted and dusty in the dry season and muddy and slippery after the rains began. It was along the route of the East African Safari Rally, considered by many to be the world's toughest car rally. It was only years later that a tarmac road was built westwards from Nairobi towards the Uganda border.

Despite the journey's privations, I was thrilled and excited to be in

Kenya. The country was throbbingly alive. My travelling companions were cheery and once we had descended into the Rift Valley we began seeing occasional giraffes, stiff legged in gait and their long necks swaying, nibbling on roadside thorn trees. The journey took two days, stopping overnight in the middle of Kenya's tea-growing area, its lush dark green hills criss-crossed by *murram* tracks as we sped along leaving a long trail of thick red dust behind.

I arrived after two days at Kakamega, headquarters of Western Region, where the governor, dressed in a semi-military uniform of khaki trousers and bush shirt, asked me a few questions before sending me onwards 60 miles to Kolanya in his official car. Kenya was beginning to live up to expectations!

I was met by Kolanya Secondary School's ginger-haired headmaster, a Salvation Army officer from England. The Salvation Army had founded the school, and also ran a nearby small clinic, but it was in the process of Africanisation and actually had two head teachers, the other a Kenyan who was also the history teacher waiting for the Englishman's retirement. While many local people had adopted Christianity, they still had their own traditional beliefs pre-dating the arrival of Christianity. Instead of morning prayers, for instance, the charming custom remained among the elderly of spitting each morning towards the rising son while uttering, in Teso, *Akalong ngari giny*, or 'God take care of us.'

The Salvation Army head broke the news to me that I would not after all be deputy head. Although his Kenyan deputy was very ill and I would be taking over his duties as an English master, school and national politics dictated that he would be kept on in his position. I was philosophical about it. There was nothing I could do and I had been briefed by the Ministry of Overseas Development briefing to expect different social mores in Kenya than in Britain. For example, we were advised, and it proved true, that Kenyan teachers were obliged to give about half of their meagre salaries to members of their extended families, especially to cover the costs of schooling for children, often extending to 20 or more small souls.

I shared a quite substantial bungalow with a young Peace Corps volunteer, Paul Killough, head of the physics and chemistry department, a post I inherited on his departure. Meanwhile, as well as teaching English I also taught geography and a bit of science. We had a bedroom each, a comfortable living room with a substantial fireplace and quite a good library of books, a shower room and a tiny kitchen with a stove powered by a gas canister and a little gas fridge. Electric lights were generated for part of the day, but there was no mains electricity or TV.

I had also been advised by the Ministry back in Britain that, whatever I felt about the rights and wrongs of hiring house servants, I would be expected by the locals to do so and that I should pay them at the same £5 a month rate as paid by my African teacher colleagues. This might not seem a lot, but it was 10 per cent of my salary. I actually hired a house boy and a *shamba* boy as well, so 20 per cent of my income went on servants' wages. The now politically incorrect term 'boy', which then was universally used and continues to be widely used, applied even to male servants old enough to be one's grandfather.

A *shamba* is a smallholding or vegetable garden, and every teacher at Kolanya was given a half-acre of land on which to grow their own food or graze a cow or two. The produce from my land – sweetcorn, tomatoes, carrots, potatoes, onions, aubergines, peppers and lettuce – did very well and was shared with my servants who, given the lack of modern amenities, were indispensable. We made our own breakfasts and cooked our own suppers, but we needed someone to clean, shop in the local market and prepare lunch.

Our milk, delivered daily in a little aluminium can from a local *shamba*, was creamy, frothy and fresh from the cow, although it had a faint pungency. During the dry season a neighbour said she had discovered that the farmer was so scared of losing our custom when his cow ran a bit dry that he had been peeing in the milk to top up the volume. She told him we would rather have less milk than the urine-enhanced version and would be happy to keep his payments at the same level. I was amused that I had unwittingly taken up a practice, urine drinking, that is highly recommended by some health fanatics. One of my heroes, Mahatma Gandhi, drank his own urine. It is not an enthusiasm I share, but I understand it is an extremely good antiseptic and that if you receive a wound on a jungle expedition the best thing to do in the absence of other medication is to pee on it.

The school had an old broken tractor we were meant to be able to use on our *shambas*. Paul Killough got the tractor going again and showed me how to maintain it. I learned to strip a gearbox, check the hydraulics, work on the big and little ends, realign wheels, and strip out and reline the brake pads. Because so much sand got into the carburettor during the dry season, I learned how to strip it down to its components in the dark, clean it and rebuild it within 20 minutes. I could have completely reassembled a tractor from its component parts. I had arrived as a schoolteacher: by the time I returned to Britain I was also a mechanic and farmer.

Mechanical wizard though I became, I had huge difficulty passing my Kenyan driving test. I had bought a hardy little Renault 4L, known in Kenya as 'the poor man's Land Rover'. The 4L could cope with steep hills and the muddiest of roads. If it got stuck it took only two or three people to lift it out. I took my first driving test in Bungoma, near the Uganda border about 30 miles from where I was teaching. The examiner was a huge African with a military bearing who had served in the Royal Air Force as a gunner in Lancaster bombers during the Second World War. I was so nervous at the start of the test that I had difficulty in getting the 4L started. We had not gone far when he said: 'Stop. I am failing you for turning the ignition key the wrong way.'

Driving into Bungoma for my second attempt to get my Kenyan licence, I noticed one of my lights was broken. Rather than be failed for that, I borrowed a friend's 4L. But half way through the test the car ran out of petrol. I walked back to the test offices in stony silence with the same furious-looking examiner, who failed me once again.

The third time a young Dutch nurse in a local hospital gave me a tranquilliser of the kind taken by violinists to calm their nerves before a performance. I sat on a bench in the sun with about 10 young Africans all awaiting our fate. Testing day was something of a local event, equivalent to a bull fight. Crowds turned up to encourage and commiserate enthusiastically as each victim took his or her place behind the wheel. We saw the examiner – same chap – advancing towards us in a truck along the red *murram* roads. He was bouncing along at 40 miles per hour, kicking up great clouds of dust, with a young African in the back being jerked off his feet every time the truck went over the many deep ruts. At every bump the passenger's terrified face appeared above the back of the driving cab goggle-eyed with airborne fear. The examiner skidded to a halt and had a face like thunder as he slammed the truck door and strode towards us. Thank goodness for the pill. At the third attempt, I sailed through the test.

We had to clear the undergrowth around the school regularly, and on one occasion a group of friends and pupils killed 250 cobras. One of the kids gave me a cobra skin which I have to this day. They also brought me tarantula spiders, of which there are many varieties, most of them big, hairy and superficially scary. All tarantulas, also known in Africa as baboon spiders, are venomous, but only some species have poison that can produce extreme discomfort over a period of several days. Legend apart, tarantula bites are not known to have resulted in human fatalities. Most are either busy minding their own business or are so harmless that they have sadly entered the exotic pet trade.

Regardless of their fearsome reputation, tarantulas are themselves an object of predation. A pair of tarantula hunters were given to me by my pupils one day – a magnificent female Verreaux's Eagle-owl and her chick. Now, this is no tiny bird. The world's third largest owl, the adult stands some two-and-a-half feet high with a wing span of more than six feet. Besides large spiders, a Verreaux's Eagle-owl also eats birds, monkeys, mongoose, frogs, fish and carrion.

I do not know where the kids got the birds or why they gave them to me. Perhaps they thought they would be useful additions to the biology lab, either alive or stuffed? The only thing I could think to do with them was put the Eagle-owl and her chick on a table close to an open window so they could regain their freedom. The mother bird, her light grey feathers patterned with small black barring, flew off and did not return, leaving me with a weeks-old orphan Verreaux's Eagle-owl chick whom I named Nebuchadnezzar, or Neb for short because he was all beak.

I used to sleep on the floor on a mattress, having first poisoned all the giant cockroaches that infested my house. The slaughter was necessary, otherwise I would have lived cheek by jowl with creatures that contaminate food, spread germs, leave foul odours and damage books and other personal possessions. There were thousands of cockroaches which – all my green credentials notwithstanding – I found vile. They inhabited all manner of spaces, their long quivering antennae poking out of every crack. They had malignant, fiery eyes and in dim light they looked as big as mice. I eventually eliminated them by putting down poison regularly at the base of all my doors. In the cockroach-free zone near my bed, I made Neb a little nest. With the help of my cook, I fed him scraps day and night. He used to hop across the floor to nibble my ear to wake me in the morning when he was hungry. I could find no advice about what I should really be feeding him. Sadly, Neb did not thrive and died after ten days.

On another occasion I found a horse in my living room. I had returned from a morning of teaching to eat lunch before having a short siesta. It was a beautiful glossy chestnut gelding hunter belonging to the wife of my head of department. I suspect it had wandered in through the patio doors to get into some shade on a very hot day. My main concern was to get it out before it began relieving itself all over the place. It was far too big to be pushed out, so in the end I went around the house, gathered a bundle of grass and lured it back out of the living room and across the patio into the open air.

The same lady kept a goat which escaped one day and got into my *shamba*. In the space of a morning it was as though a giant electric razor had passed over my crops. The *shamba* was bare, my tomatoes, onions, lettuce and other vegetables chopped down so that all that remained were a few half inch-high stumps. I would gladly have killed and roasted that animal.

*　　*　　*

Teaching ran largely on skates because the kids' thirst for knowledge was so great. I say 'kids', but many of the students were well into their twenties, and I was only 28, and some were married with kids. Some were more than six feet tall and I would never have dared threaten any of them with a Lochgelly Number Three!

While some walked up to 14 miles to and from school each day, most lived in term-time in the hostels. I got to know the hostel-dwellers well because, after the electricity generator was switched off in the early evening, they continued studying by paraffin lamps. When doing my night rounds, ostensibly to make sure lamps had been extinguished and all were in bed, I would squat on the floor helping them with their physics and chemistry, chalking on the concrete.

The going, however, was not all smooth. Teaching chemistry was, well . . . interesting. Many of the pupils had never seen an electric light switch outside the school, let alone a Bunsen burner, test tube, petri dish or acids and alkalis. The chemistry lab was well equipped and one of the first things I had to do was explain carefully rules about safety. One of these was that only very small quantities of acid, alkalis, salts and metals needed to be used in experiments. The problem was to restrain them from using a teaspoonful of a substance rather than a few grains on the tip of a spatula. Before one practical examination I hoped they would remember everything I had taught them. Wrong! Halfway through the second exam experiment the lab filled with such dense clouds of chlorine gas that it looked like a First World War trench under a gas assault. The exam had to be stopped, all the windows opened and the lab evacuated. Luckily, there was a slight breeze and after a quick wash of all the test tubes the exam continued. I am happy to say that the school got the best Oxford and Cambridge Schools Examination Board science result it had ever had.

Things could get quite serious on occasions. Late one evening, an hour after we had turned off the generator, we heard a rumpus on the other side of the school compound and the sound of pebbles rattling on a tin roof. A very worried pupil knocked at the door and began telling Andrew Okumo, the teacher with whom I was now sharing the house following the departure of Paul, that boys were stoning the house of the Salvation Army headmaster. The mood was angry and getting worse.

The full deadly seriousness of the situation was immediately clear to Andrew and me. Three weeks earlier, a similar incident had occurred just across the border in Uganda. A well-loved British teacher had been stoned to death by pupils when he tried to intervene in what was a food riot.

Andrew and I acted swiftly. While I turned on the generator, flooding the compound with light, Andrew with considerable courage moved among the rioters and persuaded them to assemble in the classrooms so that they could explain to us what was troubling them. I went round the dormitories and told those who were not taking part in the riot also to gather in the classrooms.

Their story was the same as that which had led to the grisly murder of the teacher in Uganda. For most of the past month they had been given very little to eat other than *posho*, maize flour cooked with water to a porridge- or dough-like consistency. By itself, *posho* is relatively inexpensive but of low nutritional value. Rural Kenyans, however, roll a lump of *posho* into a ball with their fingers and dip it into a sauce or stew of vegetables or meat or both, using the *posho* as a scoop. The pupils wanted a little chicken or meat with their *posho* at least twice a week together with gravy and some vegetables from the school's own *shamba*.

Neither Andrew nor I had known of the food grievance, which seemed to us entirely justified, but we pleaded with them to be patient until morning when we said we would ensure that the headmaster received a student deputation to listen to their complaint. Normal service and peace were restored. The appalling diet had been a matter of pure mismanagement and incompetence by the school's tortuous administrative system. The headmaster failed to make an appearance at any time throughout the previous evening, and in retrospect it was a matter of luck that our swift intervention had worked.

Less serious was an incident with a singing gardener in a nearby *Harambee*[2] self-help rural school of a type that sprang up with unqualified teachers throughout Kenya after independence from Britain in 1963. The children were sitting their Kenya Junior Certificate of Education exam and were being supervised by a British teacher from another school. Silence prevailed, apart from the cheerful loud singing of the school gardener cutting dry grass in the outside grounds. The supervisor found the singing deeply irritating and worried himself that it might affect the children's concentration, but he could not leave the

[2] *Harambee* in Swahili means 'all pull together'.

room unsupervised to go outside to complain. Some weeks later he learned that the children had all achieved excellent results, largely because the 'gardener', who in fact proved to be a teacher who had got hold of the examination papers, had been singing to them answers to the exam questions in *Teso*. The results stood.

* * *

At Kolanya I had a tremendous sense of being in a young country. Although I was in Teso tribal country, the pupils came from a mixture of Kenya's more than 70 different tribal groups. One day a pupil was trying to identify his friend to me and said: 'You know, Mr Harper, that is the one who is very black.' I began looking at the pupils' skin colours more carefully the next day, and they varied from the lightest of olive browns to intense blue-black.

Besides science teaching and riot control, I coached football and athletics and banged the big drum in the school's Salvation Army band at morning assembly while singing hymns in Swahili. I launched a debating society in which all the main speakers assumed positions in government followed by votes. Nearly every pupil wanted to be either a lawyer or a professional politician, because that was where the best money could be earned or gleaned. We did not have a technical teacher and there were only two or three technical schools in the whole of Kenya. The country simply was not producing skilled farmers or technicians. Kenya had inherited from the British colonial era an academic educational system of about 200 schools designed to train a civil service, judiciary and bureaucracy. This left a huge technical training and skills gap that is still there. Most of the garages, because of this educational shortcoming, were owned or run by Asians. The lack of routine maintenance, as well as the poor levels of technical expertise, could sometimes be disastrous. Just across the border at Tororo in Uganda the roof of the country's biggest cement factory collapsed. There had been no simple routine sweeping of cement dust from the roof. Many tonnes of it accumulated and during the rains it solidified and the roof caved in.

The potential was there, if all other things had been equal, for Kenyans to shine in science and technical subjects. Sammy Kiduyu was perhaps the most brilliant pupil I have ever taught. He was about 18 and so quick with maths that I used to ask him for help. Together, he and I gave private lessons. In one maths exam Sammy scored 100 per cent. I faced a philosophical problem – because there is no such thing as mathematical perfection, 100-per cent certainties do not exist. So I explained to Sammy that I was awarding him only a 99.5 per cent mark. He looked a bit mystified.

One of my other projects was to transform the school library, which was packed with tonnes of medical journals and advanced Western histories donated by an American university with absolutely no relevance whatsoever to Africa. There was not a single book by an African author. So, on a trip to Nairobi I went to the main bookshop, blew part of my salary on a shelf of African-authored books and once back in Kolanya ran a free lending library out of my house. I was convinced, correctly I believe to this day, that they needed Ngugi wa Thiong'o[3] more than Charles Dickens.

When a science-qualified Kenyan teacher arrived at Kolanya, I was transferred to another school, Amakura Secondary, right on the border with Uganda, where I taught history and English. The first term I was there began two weeks late because there were no mattresses for the hostel beds. My blackboard was a wall that had been painted black. It was a Catholic school and the head was a Kenyan priest who was in line for a bishopric. Father Okodi's nickname was Scorch because whenever there was trouble in the school he would jump into his VW car and 'scorch' across the border into Uganda until someone else had solved the problem.

Despite his propensity for fleeing trouble, Father Okodi had a saintly manner, which is more than can be said for some of the local British residents, a mixture of aid workers, farm owners and teachers. The community was a mini Happy Valley, riddled with sexual intrigues. I shared a house at Amakura with another Peace Corps guy, as lacking in gravity as Paul Killough was deeply serious, who

---

[3] Ngugi is Kenya's and East Africa's greatest author. *Weep Not, Child, A Grain of Wheat* and *Petals of Blood* have been translated into more than 30 languages. Ngugi's writing is critical of both colonial-era Kenya and also the post-independence governments.

was constantly high on the drawer full of hashish he bought locally. At least he was always happy!

* * *

One of the joys of living in East Africa was escaping to game parks during holidays. My younger brother Euan joined me on one of these trips shortly after he had qualified as a commercial airline pilot. To celebrate his arrival with a barbecue, I bargained in Swahili in a local market to buy a sheep and bundled it live into the back of my small Renault 4L. In exchange for a share of the meat, it was slaughtered by a couple of Kikuyus who knew how to use every part of the carcass, including making some fantastic sausages. A substantial part of the carcass and some of the sausages were roasted back at Kolanya.

In Uganda's Queen Elizabeth National Park Euan and I were charged by a hippo, an animal which takes more human lives than any other in Africa, which narrowly missed the 4L. We travelled on to the Mountains of the Moon, on the Congo border, to try to track and walk with mountain gorillas. We gazed at smoking volcanoes and down into beautiful cloud-dotted jungle valleys, but sadly we met no gorillas. In Kenya's Tsavo National Park I stopped the car to look at an elephant. When its ears began flapping I decided to get moving. It did not seem that dangerous, but I later heard that an entire Asian family had been killed in Tsavo when an angry jumbo stamped their car flat. Just before Euan left we got to the coast at Malindi, slept on the beach and woke to the sound of lapping waves and the sight of the sun rising over the Indian Ocean.

One Easter holiday Paul Killough and I took the entire Kolanya fourth year on an adventure trip by train some 700 miles to Mombasa, also on the Indian Ocean. It remains one of the great travel experiences of my life. Paul, a slightly short-sighted ginger-haired American who dressed in very long blue shorts, was a delightful man who, despite the fact that he took everything very, very seriously, used to amuse me greatly. He was so worried about maintenance on the East African Railways system that he took a small hammer with him and at each of the many stops struck the wheels of the carriages and the Manchester-built steam engines to make sure they were not cracked. East African

Railways were particularly well run at that time – although the system has since declined badly – and happily Paul never did find a cracked wheel. The last time I met Paul was when I took him to a restaurant in Nairobi just before he returned to America. He was a genuine country boy and had never been in a city in the United States. Nairobi was his first experience of both cities and of Indian food, and when a plate of rice and tandoori chicken was placed in front of him his shocked reaction was: 'Hey Robin, what's this?'

We travelled overnight and most of the following day to Nairobi, stopping *en route* at a station named Equator because it was located precisely at 0 latitude. In Nairobi we stayed in a Salvation Army hostel – as we did also in Mombasa – and visited the Kibera slum on the wrong side of Government Road, the capital's main central avenue, to meet the parents of one of the pupils. Kibera, with about a million people, is today the biggest slum in Africa south of the Sahara, heavily polluted by garbage, soot, dust and other wastes and contaminated with human and animal faeces, thanks to the open sewage system. The lack of sanitation accounts for many illnesses and diseases. Crime is rife, and unemployment rampant. It remains an illegal settlement. That means there are no title deeds, no sewage pipes, no roads . . . no services of any kind.

Kibera, even in 1968 when it was less densely populated, was pretty scary. Ten of the biggest teenagers formed a protective phalanx around us as we picked our way over the ditches and around the rubbish and excrement. It did seem extraordinary that there was some sort of organisation amidst the chaos. Laughter was everywhere and we were received with hugs and warm smiles. The children were for the most part clean and well dressed. A friend of mine at the Royal Society of Arts, the Poland-born London architect Cezary Bednarski, has designed low-cost, socially sustainable houses for Kibera. His plans are wonderful and I hope to get involved with them.

We travelled onwards towards the coast at a mere 25 miles per hour because, although the carriages and engines of the East African Railways are large, the single track is narrow gauge. Speed is out of the question, especially around bends. Built by the British to carry raw materials out of the Uganda colony and to carry manufactured

British goods back in, the first East African Railways train ran in 1901. Construction was carried out principally by Sikh labourers brought in from British India: many remained in Africa to create the substantial Indian minority communities in Kenya and Uganda. Man-eating lions were a major hazard during construction, and estimates range up to 135 for the number of men killed by the big cats in attacks on the workers' camps.

In Mombasa a local church laid on a bus to take us to a beach north of the city. The kids were impressed by the sea's apparent vastness and all of them stripped to their underpants and dashed into the Indian Ocean waves with cries of joy. Almost as quickly they ran back up the beach spitting and spluttering and begging for water. It was a good combined geography and chemistry lesson, of the practical kind I favour, about sea water's saltiness. My lasting memory is of the children exclaiming, once they had drunk great quantities of fresh water, 'That was so very salty, Mr Harper! Please, why is the water so salty?'

* * *

I had a girlfriend in Uganda, Jenny Cohen, the step-daughter of one of the last British colonial governors, Sir Andrew Cohen, who helped prepare Uganda for independence. Visiting her at weekends, I used to cross into Uganda through a leper colony where there were no border controls. One of Jenny's friends was a senior official in a United Nations organisation, who invited us to a big reception in Kampala, the Ugandan capital. We were chatting to Prime Minister Milton Obote when someone pointed out a big man in army uniform across the room and said: 'Don't go anywhere near that man. He's very dangerous.' He was Idi Amin, who overthrew Obote in 1971 and established military rule for eight years, during which time there was political repression, ethnic persecution, extrajudicial killings, corruption and gross economic mismanagement. The number of people killed by Amin's regime has been estimated by international observers and human rights groups to range between 100,000 and 500,000.

My last visit to Uganda happened 18 months after Jenny Cohen and I had gone our separate ways. I was on my way back to Britain from

Kenya and the East African Airways DC-10 had made a stop at Kampala's Entebbe Airport to refuel and pick up passengers. Shortly after take-off, I noticed with alarm that fuel was streaming across the port (left) wing. The captain announced that fuel was being jettisoned to lighten the plane so that we could return to Entebbe. No explanation was given. On landing, we were hauled off the plane by intimidating-looking security men in dark glasses and brown raincoats who grunted orders at us. When we reboarded, some passengers did not return.

We learned that a state of emergency had been declared. Someone had tried to assassinate Obote, shooting him through the jaw and both cheeks, removing a number of teeth. Two youths from the southern Buganda tribe were arrested and convicted, but Obote refused to sign their death sentences. Many suspected that Amin was the ultimate conspirator behind the attempted killing.

15

Not enough fish in the sea

A single modern industrial super-trawler with a crew of eight hauls in as many fish from the North Sea in nine months as the entire Dutch fleet of 1,000 boats with 10,000 crewmen caught in more than a year in the 17th century.[1] The Dutch built a worldwide empire on the proceeds of those resources.

But we are now stripping out the very last of the fish we will ever see in what was once one of the world's richest fishing grounds. The 290,000-square-mile North Sea has been exploited in a particularly ruthless way and is now a mere shadow of the extraordinarily productive system it once was.

Large sturgeon migrated up its surrounding rivers to spawn and were caught as recently as the last century. Delicious cod fried in batter with chips was almost the British national dish. It was cheap food, but cod is now an expensive delicacy. Cod grew to a full age of more than 15 years, and sometimes more than 25, a length of more than two metres (six feet) and a weight of 90 kgs (200 pounds). European Union scientists calculate that 93 per cent of North Sea cod are now fished before they reach breeding age and that 88 per cent of all EU fish stocks are over-fished.

Until recently, there was one stock, North Sea plaice, which seemed to be able to withstand the enormous over-fishing pressure. But this too has fallen below the minimum safe population size. Plaice fishermen, especially those from Holland, plough the seabed with heavy net gear and leave underwater lunar landscapes in their wake. Skate has

[1] This was noted by Professor T.C. Smout, one of Britain's most distinguished historians, who pioneered the new discipline of environmental history studies and is now Professor Emeritus in History at St Andrews University.

virtually disappeared from the North Sea: worse still, the bodies of the few that are still caught are thrown back into the sea and all that is landed are the fleshy wings of this particular fish.

Blue-fin tuna, feeding on herring, were until about 1960 still present in the North Sea in large enough numbers to support a fishery, but are now long gone. Fishing boats today dump tonnes of dead fish overboard like garbage when they do not have a commercial licence for them. This so-called 'bycatch' totals some million tonnes annually of dead and wasted fish. These discards amount to about one-third of the total annual catch in the North Sea, according to the Worldwide Fund for Nature (WWF).

The North Sea historically has been nature's gift to the European nations whose shores line it. Its future now is bleak indeed. So what, if anything, can be done to save our sea?

For a start, we need to stop all the double-talk about commercial fishing and drain off the oceans of misinformation. Not many fishermen seem concerned about exercising self-restraint as the looming environmental catastrophe hurtles towards them. The fishing industry constantly complains that under European Union regulations the number of boats permitted to fish in the North Sea is steadily declining. This grumble disguises the fact that older boats are being replaced by ever-bigger boats that with modern technology land ever-bigger hauls on single trips. The total fishing capacity of the Scottish and European Union fleets is some three times greater than is necessary if we are to have any hope of reducing the North Sea fish harvest to a sustainable level.

Just before Christmas each year an EU Council of Fisheries Ministers is held in Brussels and the EU's fisheries experts release an annual report on the Common Fisheries Policy. Thanks to successive British governments' faint-hearted support for the great European adventure, which has seen the countries of the Union maintain peace between themselves for nearly 70 years, the longest period in their histories, the people of Scotland and Britain have only the sketchiest of understanding how the EU works. Most believe that 'Brussels bureaucrats' dictate European laws, known as regulations, many of which override laws passed by Westminster and Holyrood. This is a total fallacy. In fact, the fisheries laws, for example, are decided upon by the Fishing and Agriculture Ministers from each of the 27 EU states meeting in Council. The 'Brussels bureaucrats' merely implement laws decided collectively by our elected governments. It is one of the saddest sights in EU politics to watch faint-hearted squadrons of fisheries ministers spend time fishing for votes rather than voting for fish. Abjectly subservient to the fishing industry, they lack all courage and play it short term, doing what they know what must be wrong and every year permitting more fish to be taken out of the sea than makes sense.

The fishing community itself protests about reductions in the total allowable catch (TAC)[2] and then when it itself undermines those same rules it says they do not work. They plead poverty, but still attract investment. A friend of mine in northeast Scotland sold a hotel to a fisherman who put £50,000 in cash on the hotel bar as a down payment. One fisherman I know was able to borrow his first £2 million for a new boat when he was aged only 22. Our banks, who we now know loaned irresponsibly on the housing market, also fed the over-fishing of the North Sea. At Peterhead, Scotland's and Britain's main fishing port, more Porsche cars are crashed every year than anywhere else in Scotland.

Fishing captains and owners like to portray themselves as extremely brave men putting their lives in peril to provide us with fish. Yes, the sea can be very dangerous and we must respect the tenacity and nerve of those who take the risks. But we also need to strip away false sentiment. Men venture into this work because the rewards can be great. Aboard a properly maintained large modern trawler the risks are minimal compared to life on boats 50 years ago and to those faced today on smaller fishing vessels. The people who take the greatest risks are the deckhands, and most of these are imported labourers from the Philippines – there are 900 Filipinos on British fishing boats.

I want to see our few remaining fishing communities survive at a sustainable level and I want to see our fish stocks recover to the point

---

[2] A TAC is the maximum quantity of fish that can be caught from a specific stock over a given period of time. At negotiations in December each year in Brussels TACs are shared among EU states according to national quotas.

where at some time in the future we may be able to entertain the idea of increasing the fishing capacity of our fleet. Meanwhile, the EU fisheries experts would like to see the Union's fishing fleet capacity slashed by 70 per cent to get on top of the crisis. That would be a good start. Governments should simply buy out enough boats to reach the target. We should then also begin landing the million tonnes per year of fish that are thrown back into the North Sea, thanks to the laws made by our fishing ministers. That would make it possible to gain much more scientifically accurate assessments of what fish are surviving where and what is the state of the stocks.

Four times more fish were being landed in British ports 100 years ago than today. Catches peaked in 1938, when they were more than five times heavier than catches made with today's infinitely more sophisticated fishing vessels and technological aids. That figure alone sends out an alarming Doomsday warning. 'For all its technological sophistication and raw power, today's trawl fishing fleet has far less success than its sail-powered equivalent of the late 19th century because of the sharp declines in fish abundance,' according to Ruth Thurstan, of York University's Environment Department, one of three co-authors of a 2010 report in the journal *Nature Communications* on the dire state of our fish stocks.

Simon Brockington, another *Nature Communications* report co-author and head of conservation at the Marine Conservation Society, a British charity dedicated to the protection of the sea environment and its wildlife, said: 'More than a century of intensive trawl fishing has severely depleted UK seas of bottom-living fish like halibut, turbot, haddock and plaice.'

The third co-author, Callum Roberts, an internationally renowned Professor of Marine Biology at York University, said the levels and conditions of European and global fish stocks are far worse than even the most pessimistic of modern assessments. 'The current relentless exploitation of fish stocks means that all we exploit today will have collapsed completely by 2050,' he said. 'We absolutely have to set aside sea area habitats in which life can re-establish itself, where ecosystems can recover health from centuries of over-fishing.'

The *Nature Communications* study concluded:

It is clear that seabed ecosystems have undergone a profound reorganisation since the industrialisation of fishing and that commercial stocks of most bottom-living species, which once comprised an important component of marine ecosystems, collapsed long ago.[3]

Similar studies had long beforehand convinced me that a revolutionary approach to fish stocks conservation was vital and that the Scottish Parliament should use its powers to establish marine conservation reserves around our shores from which all commercial fishing needs to be banned. The health of the North Sea had been one of the top items on my agenda even before I made the Green Party parliamentary breakthrough in 1999.

The only way we in the Green Party could hope to obtain an act to protect our seas was to convince other groups that it was necessary: we had to preach beyond the converted. I was determined to bang on about it until the state of our seas and fish stocks became not just my preoccupation but that of the mainstream parties also.

The piece of evidence that perhaps most comprehensively suggested a public mood change, and a boost for our ideals, came when *The Scotsman*, which promotes itself as Scotland's national newspaper, began campaigns to 'Save Our Seas' and persuade the nation to 'Go Green'.

It was an extraordinary but welcome flip-flop by *The Scotsman* following a change of ownership and a dire period of grim years. During these, under the previous ownership and its extreme right-wing editor-in-chief Andrew Neil, the newspaper's longstanding liberal ethos had been trashed in favour of a deeply reactionary agenda that was anti-conservation. It involved the abolition of the post of environment correspondent and the dismantlement of the investigative unit. *The Scotsman* became virulently and unintelligently anti-Europe; out of touch with most Scottish opinion; and over-the-top critical of the Scottish Parliament. The paper, almost entirely negative about all

---

[3] 'The effects of 118 years of industrial fishing on UK bottom trawl fisheries,' by Callum Roberts, Ruth Thurstan and Simon Brockington, *Nature Communications*, 4 May 2010.

the era's great challenges, suffered a drastic drop in circulation which to this day has not recovered despite a change of ownership and the migration of Neil to London.

The 'new' *Scotsman*'s Save Our Seas campaign called for a comprehensive system of marine planning and for the establishment of a network of marine reserves. While our waters contained some of the most precious marine environments in the world, the campaign highlighted the fact that they were almost completely unprotected from human exploitation.

Among other proposals, *The Scotsman* said marine reserves would protect fish populations, providing them with refuges where they could spawn and breed away from the pressure of industrialised fishing. It quoted York University's Professor Callum Roberts as saying:

> Extensive marine reserves are essential if we are to conserve the ocean's resources. If we wish to preserve the few unspoiled areas that we have left, then we must protect them now.

The Scotsman then went one extraordinary step further. On 9 January 2008 it changed its traditional blue masthead to green for a day and urged Scots to 'go green'. Thousands signed up to 10 pledges to lead greener lifestyles, including buying more seasonal and unpackaged food, recycling household waste and leaving the car at home more often in favour of walking or cycling to work. 'If every person in the country joined in the campaign, we could cut our energy use by as much as 40 per cent,' said the newspaper's restored environment correspondent, who went on to say:

> There is a need to change the way we live in order to fulfil the requirements of the fight against climate change. Scientists and politicians across the world are in almost unanimous agreement that the time for argument is over.

The Scotsman did not refer to the Green Party, but that hardly mattered. *The Scotsman*'s campaign vindicated all of the party's efforts to make green issues part of the mainstream political agenda. Realistically, we had never sought political power for the sake of power, but we did want to change the shape of the agenda and debate about the future of the planet and make them everyone's concern.

In its 'Go Green' edition, *The Scotsman*'s environment correspondent also wrote:

> Unless humanity takes steps to reduce greenhouse gas emissions, the world will be hit by famine, drought, floods, storms of increasing intensity and rising sea levels. How bad this will be and when it will strike may be uncertain, but a worst-case scenario would result in vast tracts of the planet becoming unsustainable, prompting mass migrations towards the poles and wars over territory.[4]

Happily and almost miraculously, the Scottish government introduced legislation to overhaul the planning system for the 1,600-mile-long Scottish coastline and its waters 200 miles out to sea and to establish conservation zones.

The Marine (Scotland) Act became law on 10 March 2010. It was a huge conservation breakthrough. From the Green Party's point of view it was far from perfect, but it was way beyond anything I could have expected immediately after I became a lone Green parliamentarian 10 years earlier. I participated frequently in the debates on the details of the bill, successfully introducing an amendment to protect grey seals and common seals from armed hunts, but failing for the time being to establish specific reserves for our rich whale and dolphin populations or to get the Scottish government to establish a seaborne police force to tackle environmental marine crime and crack down on abuses of fishing regulations.

But the Marine Act is an enabling piece of legislation which will be built upon down the decades, leading to an ever more pristine sea and coast environment. We in the Green Party regard it as one of our victories. But in truth it is a victory for all Scots, whatever the colour of their political stripes.

---

[4] 'Let's Go Green Together: Ten simple ways we can all help save the planet,' by Ian Johnston, *The Scotsman*, 9 January 2008.

16

My 'interesting!' acting career

Back in Britain after my time in Kenya, I returned to Braehead as temporary head teacher of chemistry. Mackenzie had moved on, but I was keen to teach there again and some of the children were still around who had written many letters to me in Kenya.

'Dear Mr Harper, I wish you were back in Scotland,' said one of these epistles that made me homesick as I read them on many an evening as the tropical sun set. 'Mum is asking after you. She says you've to look after yourself.' Another read: 'Do the elephants run into your house? Or is it the monkeys?' And yet another: 'How are things over there? Plenty of women for you? Do they all go about half naked like they all say they do?'

Most of my former pupils, however, had left. Without Mackenzie and without the fourth year, which had been transferred to the new local comprehensive school, reducing Braehead's numbers to just 200, it felt a different place.

With my savings I had bought my first car in Britain, a Renault 4L like the one I had owned in Kenya, although within weeks Kenya seemed like a distant memory. The 4L gave me easy access at weekends to Edinburgh, where I renewed old friendships. Among these were the budding actor-director Sandy Neilson, now a distinguished veteran thespian who is currently contracted to the Royal Shakespeare Company, and the storyteller and budding BBC drama director David Campbell.

Sandy and David wanted to stage a unique multi-arts event at the 1970 Edinburgh International Festival Fringe – plays, music, poetry readings, art exhibitions and fashion shows all under one roof. They had already lined up as performers the poets Norman MacCaig and

Hugh MacDiarmid and the superb mime and dance duo Lindsay Kemp and Jack Birkett, the latter of whom went by the stage name The Incredible Orlando. Both Lindsay and Jack were flamboyantly gay, and when Jack, who sometimes appeared on stage in black fishnet tights and pink panties, died in 2010 Lindsay wrote:

> Jack was Judy to my Mr Punch, Harlequin to my Pierrot, Titania to my Puck, Herodias to my Salomé, Queen of Hearts to my Lewis Carroll. We shared flats, dressing rooms, boyfriends, bills, good times and bad times, success and failure; a couple of extravagant young dreamers, a couple of aching elders, always entertainers.

Lindsay, one of the greatest exponents of the art of mime, was a guru to the glam-rock megastar David Bowie, who spent several years studying under Kemp before emerging in androgynous splendour in the guise of Ziggy Stardust. 'I taught David to free his body,' said Lindsay.

I was one of the financial backers of Sandy's and David's enterprise, which ran for two seasons at Edinburgh Festival time under the title The Fort Knox Arts Complex. They had hit on the name because what we were running was a pocket festival in its own right which we considered to be 'full of artistic gold'.

To my surprise, I was asked to play a leading role in a Fort Knox production of the existentialist French play *Huis Clos* by Jean-Paul Sartre, in which three deceased characters are punished by being locked in a room together for eternity, giving rise to Sartre's most famous quotation '*L'Enfer, c'est les autres* (Hell is other people).'

My previous acting experience was extremely limited. At university I had some small parts in plays, including N.F. Simpson's *One Way Pendulum*, a farce in which I played an onstage clock with a single line which I twice managed to fluff in performance. In Kenya I joined a little troupe of teachers – African, Asian and European – who had formed the Western Kenya Drama Group which toured productions in English round the region's schools. I auditioned for a part in a production of Christopher Bond's *Sweeney Todd, the Demon Barber of Fleet Street*, and got the lead role. We played in four schools over a period of two weeks, our stage lighting being the headlights from a couple of cars. As Sweeney Todd, the barber who cut his customers' throats before tipping them into the basement to be made into pies, I was booed and hissed every time I appeared on stage by the young Africans, who had a delightful facility for suspending disbelief and got personally involved in the production. This, with hindsight, was good training for my later career as a politician. When at one performance I growled and waved my razor – a fearsome length of silver-painted serrated wood – the first two rows of the audience were so terrified that they screamed and screamed and fell backwards, tipping their seats, and we had to wait for a few minutes until order was restored.

Huis Clos is a very demanding play, lasting just over an hour on stage for three people with no interval. Sandy wanted to make a little film to show the audience, before we came onstage, how the three characters had died before meeting in Hell. I lay on my back in a ruined building near St Bernard's Well on the Water of Leith, a magic little river that descends from the hills and runs through the centre of Edinburgh to the sea. Pig's blood oozed from fake bullet holes in my chest and stomach. The final shot was of one of the backstage staff dressed as a Mexican putting a pistol into my mouth to deliver the coup de grace. I was allowed a final draw on a cigarette and immediately after my brains were blown out and my head jerked backwards I let the smoke curl from my mouth.

Huis Clos was staged during the long school summer holiday. I nearly dropped out after being offered a very good job crewing a beautiful racing yacht in the Mediterranean. From Ibiza I phoned Sandy Neilson, the play's director, to try to wriggle out of the commitment. His response was so angry and withering that I reluctantly returned to Edinburgh and found myself sharing a dressing room with Lindsay Kemp, who was not in the play but performing his mime season with Jack the Great Orlando. Lindsay unashamedly had numerous boyfriends, and although he was great fun I was desperately hoping he would not fancy me. Eventually and inevitably, he asked: 'Are you one of us?' To which I said: 'I'm sorry Lindsay, no.' And to which he replied with a smile: 'Oh, pity.'

The Scotsman gave me a good personal write-up in its review of the play, and completely out of the blue I received an offer from the late Freddie Young, then one of the few active theatrical agents in Scotland, who registered my name in a huge book of out-of-work actors. This seemed to me to be the stuff that dreams are made of. The first subsequent role that Freddie, an outspoken lady whose real first name was Winifred, obtained for me was the lead male part in a Christmas children's musical. This fitted in with the school holiday, with Braehead giving me an extra week's unpaid leave so that I could perform the full run into the New Year.

My fee as the Prince and assistant stage manager in a musical version of the Brothers Grimm fairy tale *Rapunzel* at the Civic Theatre in Ayr was £8 a week. In the story the beautiful golden-haired Rapunzel is, for various reasons, shut away by an enchantress in a tower in the middle of the woods, with neither stairs nor door and only one room and one window. The lovelorn Prince turns up at the base of the tower and appeals to Rapunzel to let down her hair so he may climb the 'golden stair' towards her and ask for her hand in marriage.

The production did not go well at first, mainly because during rehearsals Rapunzel's real-life husband, the show's pianist, had to transfer to another Christmas show and was replaced, in the leading lady's view, by a much inferior substitute. When it came to our first and only duet she was sulking so intensely that she did not appear at all and I was left alone, in big beard and flowing black hair, singing towards an empty balcony at the top of the tower. It is the kind of rare situation that every thespian has to be prepared for – and improvise! I gambled that she was there somewhere at the back of the tower room and encouraged the children in the audience to shout in unison, 'Please, please Rapunzel, come and speak to the Prince.' After three repeated appeals, she shyly appeared on the balcony and we gave a particularly rousing version of the duet.

On the final night the stagehands played a practical joke. We had to set off magnesium flares to blind the audience for the scene change and then I had to utter the story's best known line – 'Rapunzel, Rapunzel, let down your golden hair.' Rapunzel then had to let down her tresses – a ship's hawser painted gold – for me to climb up towards her. As I reached towards the rope, a stage hand lifted it up beyond my reach. He did this three times before I succeeded in grabbing it. It was a musical that was meant to be played absolutely straight, but the audience was in stitches and the rest of the cast were clutching their sides in the wings.

Next, with my Equity card secured – proof that I was a legitimate actor – Freddie Young got me a part in a film, *The Massacre of Glencoe*, starring the popular actor James Robertson Justice who had just completed a four-year term as Rector of the University of Edinburgh. Freddie said the production was being financed by a Canadian with more money than sense. Unaware of how long I would be required by the director, I decided I could mess Braehead about no longer. My temporary post had only five months to run. So I took fate into my own hands, resigned and became a full-time actor. I moved to Glasgow and took lessons at the Royal Scottish Academy of Music and Drama, and learned a lot about mime from the mime artist Harry Jones.

For my role in *The Massacre of Glencoe*, I reported to Inveraray Castle, the ancestral home of the Dukes of Argyll in the Western Highlands, where the location scenes were being shot. Drinking in the bar one evening, a film executive told me that the Canadian backer was a tobacco executive, Ralph Harper. 'That's my uncle,' I said in surprise, to which I got the reply, 'Oh, then we should have given you a bigger part.' As it was, anyone who missed the first 90 seconds of the film also missed Robin Harper, aspiring famous actor.

Freddie sent me south after *Glencoe* to interview for two potential jobs in London. The first was for a Shakespeare play. I was late for the auditions and sprinted all the way along Drury Lane hurdling advertising boards to compete with 30 others for the part. I did not get it. The other was for a role as a drugged-out hippie in the avant-garde review *Oh! Calcutta!* in which the cast shocked society by appearing totally naked. Among the sketches were one about masturbation, titled 'Four in Hand', another called 'The Deflowering of Helen Axminster', and one appropriately titled, in view of my later career, 'Green-Pants, I Like the Look'. *Oh! Calcutta!* ran for 4,000 performances in London and then for 6,000 in New York. But the

Left. Orgill Cottage, at the foot of Ward Hill, Hoy, my nearly place of birth. My mother stayed here until the day I started to fight my way into this world. The doctor from HMS *Pomona* sent us both to Lyness and thence by fishing boat across the Pentland Firth to Scrabster and thence to Thurso Maternity Hospital. This drawing was done by my father just four weeks before I was born. The ashes of both Mama and Papa are scattered on Ward Hill, just behind the cottage.

Middle left. Aged three, probably taken in Gillingham, Kent.

Middle right. Me (left), aged fourteen, with my brother Euan, then aged eleven.

Above left. Aged five, taken in Orkney (note the jumper!).

Above right. Aged around five, with my parents.

Above left. Aged thirty-one, taken in St James's Park. This was my last professional photograph for my acting portfolio.

Above right. Outside Braehead school, 1967 – English teacher and musician.

Right. With my class at the Equator.

Below right. At Kamusinga Quaker High School, where I spent many happy weekends with friends.

Above left. On Mum's eightieth birthday. Left to right: Euan, Pa, Mum and myself.

Above right. Auntie Jean's eighty-fifth birthday, Manchester 1995. Left to right: Myself, David, Pa, Auntie Jean and Euan.

Left. Left to right: Myself, David, Euan.

Below left. 24 September 1994 – a very special day.

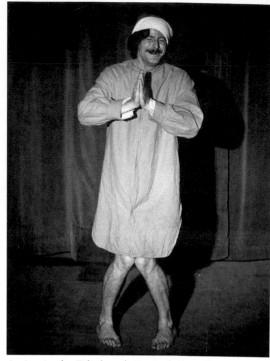

My stepson Roy marries Sarah Methven, October 2005.

Acting in the Edinburgh Festival, Fort Knox, 1972.

With students at the Dankworth Music Camp, Wavendon, near Milton Keynes.

Playing with Rhythm Method on the top of Arthur's Seat, Edinburgh.

I got my best marathon time in 1985, just outside three hours.

Singing for my supper. I gave up smoking not long after this photo was taken!

Campaigning outside Haymarket station for the European election, 1989.

At the 1989 European elections, when I notched up the first 10-per-cent vote for the Greens in Scotland.

Campaigning in Princes Street in the first Scottish Parliament elections in 1999. The green '2' played a prominent part in our campaign.

Voting in Morningside with Jenny, 6 May 1999.

Excitement as the election results are finally announced at Meadowbank Stadium, Edinburgh, around four o'clock on Friday 7 May 1999 – a full 15 hours after counting began.

My acceptance speech was very emotional – the moment overcame me!

I think everyone enjoyed the first opening of Parliament for 300 years. With Jenny in Princes Street.

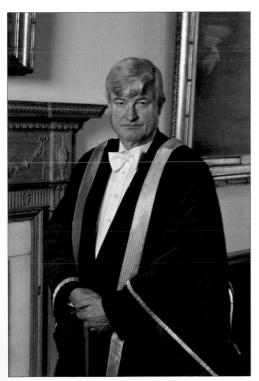

In rectorial robes. My election as Rector of Edinburgh University came as a complete surprise. (Photo: Douglas Robertson.)

A portrait taken after the 1999 election. (Photo: Douglas Robertson).

Above left. At Greenworks Scotland, a wood recycling and low carbon charity. (Photo courtesy of Stan Blackley.)

Above right. A thoughtful moment. (Photo courtesy of Callum Maclellan.)

Right. Delivering my last speech as an MSP to Party Conference. (Photo courtesy of Callum Maclellan.)

Below right. My last speech as an MSP at the Scottish Green Party Conference, in Edinburgh in October 2010, was greeted with a standing ovation. I shared the moment with Jenny. (Photo courtesy of Callum Maclellan.)

director Kenneth Tynan did not want Robin Harper appearing naked in public in either Britain or America. Neither did Robin Harper, to tell the truth. I also turned down a part as the back end of a donkey that was raped in an avant-garde drama set in a Moroccan casbah.

I did, however, secure a contract in Edinburgh with the Pool Lunchtime Theatre, an interesting venture by an Australian impresario intended to entertain the city's businessmen with short plays while they were served lunch. He was one of those wonderful people who are dedicated to theatre. A qualified pharmacist, he had worked all hours to raise the money for his venture, although he did also borrow £50 from me which I do not think he ever paid back.

The theatre-restaurant was in a Hanover Street building, in the city centre, that was due for demolition. The first play I appeared in with actress Beth Robens was a light two-hander titled *Something Beautiful Going Cheap*, set in an antique shop.

The next was too long for lunchtime and was performed in the evening. In this case, the serving of food was integral to the plot and the actors began sitting at separate tables among the diners, unknown to the customers. Diners' conversations drowned out our own opening dialogue, so we had to begin speaking in ever louder voices until they finally realised that the drama had begun.

Part of the plot involved me, as a blacked-up Bengali chef – now very politically incorrect – speaking a few words in a Bengali sing-song voice, distributing curry from a big tub together with crispy poppadoms. Before one performance we realised the production staff had failed to order the poppadoms. A furious row broke out, following which I sprinted, in full Bengali chef gear, to a nearby Indian restaurant to buy a big poppadom pile. I dashed back, balancing the poppadoms, but tripped just before my cue. The poppadoms shattered and I ended up handing to diners tiny poppadom fragments that looked more like rice crispies.

It was time to bring my short professional acting career to an end before I ended up living beneath a bridge accompanied by a few meagre possessions in plastic bags. I had sunk, and lost, my savings – including money I had put aside as a deposit to buy my first home – into trying to launch an acting career. I acted in one more Fort Knox Arts Complex season at the Edinburgh Fringe, playing Stanley in Harold Pinter's *The Birthday Party* opposite Alex Norton, then a young actor still at the Royal Scottish Academy of Music and Drama, but who has since achieved stardom in *Taggart*, the internationally famous gritty detective television drama series set in Glasgow. Alex was so fiercely and realistically aggressive at one point in the play that I completely forgot my next line. He covered for me brilliantly.

My final 1971 Fort Knox season was very hard work because I was also stage managing, doing front-of-house duties and performing music as well as acting in two dramas. My biggest achievement was to make sure that the actors were paid as we went along. The worst thing that happened was that a bundle of very expensive Victorian dresses and bodices went missing. I had collected them on behalf of the management from Kelso, in the Scottish Borders, and had promised to make sure they were returned. The theatre manager who I assisted in the final clear-up insisted that he had been given sole responsibility for the costumes and refused to let me handle them. They were put in tea chests and taken away with rubbish by dustmen never to be seen again. I have never since dared ask what the repercussions were.

In the summer term of 1971, when I was 'resting' from my acting career, I took a temporary job as a history teacher at an Edinburgh school, Leith Academy. It was an extremely happy experience and it convinced me that teaching was a more attractive long-term career proposition than the 'The Roar of the Greasepaint – The Smell of the Crowd.'[1]

As soon as that 1971 Edinburgh Festival was over I applied for and got a job teaching English in a brand new school with a very young staff at Newbattle, ten miles southeast of Edinburgh. It was a good decision since I was able to develop creatively lots of ideas I had picked up in my nine months out of full-time teaching. I subsequently taught

---

[1] The title of a successful Broadway musical by Lesley Bricusse and Anthony Newley in which Elaine Paige made her first professional appearance on stage.

for nearly 30 years and did not look back until I became a lone Green parliamentarian in 1999.

My acting career had actually added up in time to only 11 weeks of paid work, including rehearsals. I had received about £80 in fees at most and, since I never claimed social benefits, had squandered my entire savings of £800.

17

Back to teaching in 007 land

In my post-actor incarnation, I taught English for a year at Newbattle Community High School. The head of department gave me a virtual free hand, so I encouraged mime, playwriting and acting, the writing of poetry and the reading by the kids of books to each other in pairs rather than going round the class. *À la* Braehead, I started a school newspaper produced by the pupils. A few years later one of the boys approached me on an Edinburgh Street and said I had inspired him when he was just 13 years old to become a teacher himself.

Having re-entered the teaching profession, I wanted to make up for lost time. There were no gaps at Newbattle, and although I was hugely tempted by an offer to teach in Queensland, Australia, I decided against it to await an opportunity in Scotland.

While I waited for the opportunity of a breakthrough I spent the summer holiday in Majorca, where I had hoped to pursue flamenco guitar studies. The studio proved far too expensive, and I consoled myself playing guitar and singing folk, blues and jazz in Palma bars. Returning to Scotland, I accepted another temporary job, which I thought offered the chance of promotion and full-time work, at Darroch Secondary School in an industrial area of western Edinburgh in the shadow of a giant brewery. Darroch had been a pretty tough junior secondary school, thought of as a holding pen for kids until they left school at 14.

It did, however, have a very famous former pupil, Thomas Sean Connery, known as 'Big Tam'. Reputed to have been easy-going but as hard as nails, he 'graduated' in 1943 as soon as he turned 14 to become a milkman, coffin polisher and then a more successful actor than me – as MI6 agent 007 Bond, James Bond. I had just begun my first teaching job in Glasgow when in the first Bond film, 'Dr No', Sean Connery made love – and banked the first of his many millions – to Honey Rider, played by blonde-haired Ursula Andress, whose emergence from the sea in a sensational wet white bikini was voted the sexiest scene in movie history. Connery, the son of a poor factory labourer, Joe, and a domestic cleaner, Effie, was of course a legend among the Darroch kids.

Darroch had been merged with another school, James Clark, and this combined school was destined to be merged yet again with another, Boroughmuir High School. A good headmaster, with many of the qualities and aspirations of R.F. Mackenzie and better management skills, had raised Darroch from a school with the tough reputation of 007 Connery's days to a very successful high school with a strong ethos and a good public examination pass record. But the merger was badly handled by the education authorities. Both sets of pupils, from Darroch and James Clark, felt that they had been robbed of their identities and that the system was not interested in them.

On my first day at Darroch a spokesman for a group of young teachers warned me: 'Robin, this place is sheer hell. The kids never stop fighting. Any of them who show academic ability are creamed off to Boroughmuir (High School). Those who remain are an aggressive mix of children rejected by the system.'

The Darroch kids did not even like each other, never mind the teachers, because of the way they had been shaken up and tossed around by civil servants. They knew they had been unfairly treated and classes were very difficult to control. Teaching was a major challenge and I was unable to end one frenzied fight between two girls who tore each other's hair out and scattered it all around. I had to summon the janitor to prise them apart. The older staff had given up: they were just serving out their years. One was so narcoleptic that he kept falling asleep, head slumped on his desk, in front of his classes.

Happily, there was a core group of experienced and dedicated teachers who did fantastic jobs in difficult circumstances. I assured them I was well able to look after myself. As usual I was given a belt by the headmaster to use on unruly pupils. The kids saw me as a raw young recruit, not realising that I had almost a decade of experience.

One kid asked me during my first week where I had come from. 'Glasgow,' I said. They asked why I had come to Edinburgh. I lied: 'Because I was sacked after breaking a laddie's wrist with the belt.' I taught quiet, well-behaved classes for about a month after that before they cottoned on that something was not quite right. Months later, I opened one of my desk drawers and there was my hefty belt cut into six pieces with a Stanley knife, with a note attached saying: 'Sorry about this, sir, but you never used it anyway.'

One of my most difficult pupils at Darroch was a boy called David. He had a lot of problems, both in and out of school. I had huge difficulties trying to calm him down and help him get at least some benefits from an education. On one occasion he was totally out of control. Short of belting him or sending him to the headmaster, I had few weapons other than to give him a major bawling out, which I did. He reacted by calling me 'a fucking radge' in front of the whole class. 'Radge' was an urban slang word favoured by young working-class locals, and in its least obscene versions can be translated as meaning either 'a bit mental', 'an insufferable little shite', 'an idiot' – but actually much worse.

I ordered David to write a hundred lines – 'I must not call Mr Harper a fucking radge.' The next day he gave me the lines, in perfect handwriting, together with a letter from his mum castigating me for teaching her son to use bad language. I still have a copy of a fragment of those lines.

Many pupils I taught at Darroch have had troubled lives since they left school. They came from a part of the city where in successive years employment opportunities had disappeared like snow off a wall. Breweries, printing works, a whisky bond warehouse, an engineering works and a milk processing plant all closed. The area became one of Scotland's unemployment blackspots. Coupled with this was a planning blight caused by a proposal to build a giant motorway through the heart of the district to join up with Princes Street, which happily was abandoned and never revisited.

* * *

One day at Darroch I nipped out of the classroom to buy a newspaper. As I strolled back through the playground I saw chairs being eased out of the art room windows on the second floor and dropped to the playground below. It was raining chairs. I dashed upstairs and along the corridor to the art room where I saw most of the class was gathered around the elderly art master. He had been asked by the boys to give them a lesson on the use of charcoal while in the background half a dozen boys were stealthily tossing chairs out of the windows. I put a stop to it.

I knew Darroch was going to be fully incorporated into the nearby Boroughmuir High School, to which I was also due to be transferred, as part of the tide of conversion of all schools to comprehensive status. Prior to the merger, as Sean Connery's official biography put it not inaccurately:

> Toffs would go to Boroughmuir to learn languages and economics, preparing them for the professions. Big Tam and his buddies could look forward only to semi-skilled industrial labour, and were sent to Darroch to learn such skills as metalwork.

I have to confess to a bit of personal unruly vandalism just before I transferred from 007's young hunting ground to Boroughmuir. One of my favourite pupils came into my classroom at lunchtime having just bought an air rifle. I suggested that as he was in danger of being severely punished for having brought a weapon into the school that I should take care of it until dismissal time in late afternoon. I subsequently spent 15 minutes taking potshots with it at empty tin cans on top of a classroom cupboard. I would have been sacked on the spot if I had been caught. Clearing up, I discovered that one slug was buried irretrievably in the woodwork. I rationalised and comforted myself with the thought, an accurate one, that the school was falling apart anyway.

*   *   *

Boroughmuir was, and still is, a 'honeypot' school, one of the best state secondary schools in the city. Many moneyed parents tried to get their kids into Boroughmuir via the eleven-plus examination before even considering attempting to get their kids into one of Edinburgh's famous fee-paying schools – Fettes, the alma mater of former British Prime Minister Tony Blair; Edinburgh Academy, which produced Robert Louis Stevenson; Merchiston Castle; Loretto; George Heriot's; George Watson's; Stewarts Melville.

Boroughmuir, with a century-long tradition of excellence for high-attaining pupils, was dragged reluctantly into the comprehensive era. The educational and social ranges of its pupils were expanded. Students now included those allegedly destined to succeed, kids who would have passed the discredited 11-plus, and those supposedly destined to fail because they had not managed to pass the 11-plus barrier.

Beginning as assistant principal teacher of modern studies, I worked there for 27 years, three-quarters of my entire professional life. Because Boroughmuir had such strong academic and other traditions, teaching there was almost as easy as falling off a log. We worked hard to maintain the interest levels of the slower kids as much as possible, including inviting the Bay City Rollers, an Edinburgh rock band who became worldwide teen idols for a while in the 1970s, to the school to talk to and play for the pupils. I gave one of the Rollers a lesson in folk finger-style guitar-work because, in spite of their fame and success, they had only basic rock-style guitar techniques. Among my expanding interests, I helped to form the Edinburgh Classical Guitar Society; learned to play the trumpet; took violin lessons; taught guitar at the Oxenfoord Castle school for singers and accompanists near Dalkeith, south of Edinburgh; learned to fence and took over the running of the school fencing club; and became music director at Edinburgh's Theatre Workshop, a community fine arts and drama centre for children.

I also boosted my depleted savings at weekends by playing guitar and singing to diners at Henderson's Restaurant, an Edinburgh institution with an international reputation. Some evenings were huge fun, especially when other musician friends dropped in with their instruments and jammed along. For a couple of years Henderson's was a great favourite with Norwegian students who found that for the price of three beers back in Norway they could afford a bottle of champagne. They were great but noisy company and as sessions warmed up I sometimes mounted a dining table to continue my set. A huge mural adorns one of the walls at Henderson's, and there among the *glitterati* is a youthful and long-dark-haired Harper playing the guitar.

*   *   *

After ten years at Boroughmuir I began to feel stale. I was also frustrated because I had not been able to land a post as head of department. A sabbatical was out of the question, because the public education system did not allow it unless it was to return to further education to gain qualifications associated with the profession.

Boroughmuir had been one of the first schools in Britain to set up a proper guidance, or pastoral care, department. Instead of leaving the *in loco parentis* aspect of care to form teachers, it appointed a small group as guidance teachers, some of them full-time, others part-time with a reduced classroom timetable. A guidance teacher follows the progress of each student in his or her charge right through their school life, staying concerned with each student's personal, curricular and vocational welfare and keeping in close touch also with parents. I was excited by the philosophy underlying guidance education and obtained one of the part-time guidance positions.

Most of the team registered for part-time guidance studies. I took separate courses at Edinburgh University's Moray House School of Education and Jordanhill College of Education in Glasgow, obtaining a Diploma in Guidance Education.

The Boroughmuir guidance department grew and grew, with an exam-free curriculum covering relationships and sex education, health education, drugs, careers, social skills, job and college applications and a range of other matters we thought would be useful to our pupils when they entered the wider world. It taught me a lot also, especially the importance in counselling sessions of really listening rather than just hearing. It is a lesson that has been extremely useful in working with constituents in my parliamentary career.

As we developed the department, Edinburgh was just emerging from a period when it was widely depicted as the HIV/AIDS capital of Europe, largely because of the sharing of needles by drug addicts living on council estates around the city's fringes. Although this stigmatisation was unfair, the killer viral disease was spreading at an alarming rate. We therefore made AIDS education a major part of the relationships curriculum from the third year onwards.

We held discussions, showed very good videos and kept a huge box of contraceptive paraphernalia. AIDS practitioners gave talks, and whenever possible we invited HIV-positive people who were willing to talk about their experiences and how they coped with the virus. With the latter, the first lesson as far as I was concerned was to shake hands with them in front of the pupils to show I had no fear of becoming HIV-positive through normal physical contact.

The contraceptive box contained condoms, various female contraceptive devices and, with pride of place, a foot-long 'condom demonstrator', as thick as a table leg – not an actual dildo, just a small pillar of white wood. Condoms would be passed round the classroom and rolled on to the demonstrator. The condoms were blown up to demonstrate their strength or filled with water. The point was to familiarise the kids with the idea that a condom was a simple and sensible precaution to take rather than having unprotected sex with potentially drastic consequences.

The demonstrator was a vital piece of equipment, as I was reminded years later while visiting South Africa for the second Earth Summit on Sustainable Development. There I watched a performance by the brilliant satirist Pieter-Dirk Uys, son of a Jewish mother and Afrikaner father, who was touring schools telling millions of kids, in a country where a thousand people die from AIDS each day, that sex is a minefield and they must be in control of their lives. 'AIDS is the most democratic thing in the world. Everybody can get it,' he preached. 'If you can't say "no", you must use a condom.'

Uys, one of the world's funniest people, performed in theatres and schools a sketch mocking beliefs that if you put a condom on a banana and placed it on your bedside table you would be safe from conceiving or being infected with a sexually transmitted disease. After rolling a condom on to a banana, Uys said: 'No, this is not a penis,' and then, producing a black dildo that matched my own artificial phallus for size, he went on: 'THIS is a penis.'

In a country where the misplaced Calvinism of the apartheid years still resonated, Uys was accused of being 'impolite' and obscene. Responding to the sins of the racially divided past and the neglect in the present of the HIV/AIDS epidemic by the African National Congress government, Uys said:

> HIV is not a polite disease. Once upon a time, not so long ago, we had an apartheid regime in South Africa that killed people. Now we have a democratic government that just lets them die.

I would have loved to have Pieter-Dirk perform for my Boroughmuir pupils as he does for schoolchildren throughout South Africa.

* * *

The shadow of AIDS has still not lifted from Scotland. We cannot afford to be complacent, especially as the incidence of sexually transmitted diseases is growing among all ages and social classes.

Although my long sojourn at Boroughmuir ended sharply and suddenly when I was elected a professional politician, I loved the place and have since returned twice to chair debates on environmental issues and to be the guest speaker on school prize days.

18

The Greens' chance to make or break a government

I stared at the computer monitor in mounting despair. It was 2 a.m. on the morning of Friday 4 May 2007 at the Scottish Highland Showgrounds, near Edinburgh Airport, where the results of Scotland's third parliamentary election, held the previous day, were being collated.

Hundreds and hundreds of spoilt ballot papers were appearing, fuelling the Green Party's fears that the ruling Labour Party had successfully plotted to confuse voters. By the time of the final tally, some 142,000 votes – seven per cent of the national total – had been discounted, mainly because of errors made by voters.

Much of the confusion was caused because voters were asked for the first time to enter their two-vote choices – for constituency parliamentarians and for those from regional lists by proportional representations – on a single ballot paper. In the previous two elections, votes had been cast on two separate ballot papers, one coloured purple, the other peach. The new ploy was a deliberate one to undermine the Green Party's very successful 'Vote Green 2' campaign. The Labour administration switched the order of the columns on the paper, so that when voters had cast their 'first' vote and looked for Green on the second vote – which was now for first-past-the-post candidates, not 'second vote' list candidates – there were no Green names. It was a shameful and cynical piece of manipulation and had a shameful outcome, depriving my party of seats in Parliament it would otherwise have won.

Confusion was compounded by a separate ballot paper for local council elections on the same day using a different voting system which asked voters to use numbers to indicate their preferences rather than a cross, as in the parliamentary ballot.

The number of spoilt ballots caused severe delays for counts across Scotland as election night and the following day descended into chaos. BBC Scotland's political editor Brian Taylor described the situation as a disgrace.[1]

An international observer of the election said the mess was 'totally unacceptable'. Robert Richie, executive director of US-based Fair Vote, a campaign group whose aims are summed up in its name, said the difficulties amounted to Scotland's version of the 'hanging chads' fiasco in Florida which marred the 2000 US presidential election. 'The most fundamental flaw was the ballot design of the party and constituency votes in two columns on the same page, rather than on separate pages,' said Richie.

Another extraordinary error by Jack McConnell, the First Minister of the retiring Labour administration, permitted parties to put the name of national leaders on ballots for the regional list proportional representation votes. So, in my constituency, Edinburgh and the Lothians, the name of Alex Salmond, leader of the Scottish National Party (SNP), appeared on the ballot even though he was not a candidate in the constituency.

Salmond is a formidable politician and campaigner, and he was able to exploit fully his name appearing on the first part of the main ballot forms as 'Alex Salmond for First Minister' throughout the country. If an SNP administration had invented the system, it would have been seen as gerrymandering. As it was, we had to assume it was just plain stupid of the Labour government and deeply damaging to the democratic process. If this fiasco – part of it deliberate, part of it, to stretch kindness to its limits, the consequence of ineptitude – had been played out in a more populous and powerful country it would have been an international scandal of spectacular proportions.

By 5 a.m. on 4 May I realised we had lost five of our seven seats in Parliament. With Patrick Harvie in Glasgow, I was one of only

---

[1] 'Elections marred by vote problems,' BBC, 4 May 2007.

two Green MSPs re-elected. The other five lost their seats mainly because last time they had been elected with slender majorities. This made them incredibly vulnerable, especially to the SNP which focused huge effort on its campaign for the second vote. Computer modelling by Weber Shandwick, one of Britain's leading public and parliamentary relations agencies, showed that every time a few extra seats for the Scottish National Party was entered into the model, the Green Party was the first to suffer – and that is precisely what had happened.

By six in the morning I was thinking of resigning. Looking back to the first Parliament, when I was the lone Green MSP, I was not certain that I could muster the necessary physical and emotional energy to repeat the performance all over again. Mark Ballard, who had danced on the counting hall tables when elected on the second vote in Edinburgh in 2003, was now completely downcast as it became clear he would not be returning to Parliament. Briefly, I considered giving up my seat to Mark, but the procedure would have been too complicated. So I dismissed the thought and geared myself up for an acceptance speech in which I would have to drag something positive from the cold ashes.

Happily, events gave me something gloriously positive to say. Although our representation in Parliament had been reduced, we had made a significant breakthrough in local council elections. Eight Green Party candidates had been elected, five to Glasgow Council and three to Edinburgh Council – among the latter my office manager, Alison Johnson, and my researcher, Steve Burgess.

Throughout 2003–2007 Green Party democratic representation had been top-heavy, with seven elected parliamentarians and no grassroots local councillors. We could not realistically consider ourselves embedded in Scottish politics until the electorate began returning Green Party representatives at the local level. In neighbouring England and Wales, where the Green Party's one Westminster parliamentarian was elected only as late as 2010, the party had laid solid foundations for political success well beforehand by electing more than one hundred councillors and a scattering of Green mayors.

I said in my speech that in 2003 the public had elected only seven

Green Party representatives, all in Parliament. Now voters had elected 10 of us to power. From now onwards one of our top objectives had to be to ensure that we got Green Party representatives elected to local councils again and again and again.

With all the election results in, I finally returned home with my wife Jenny at about 7 p.m. on Friday 4 May. The phone was ringing as we walked in the door. It was Alex Salmond. Having achieved the slenderest possible victory he was already gearing up the SNP campaign to form a government – but he desperately needed Green Party support.

In the new Parliament, the SNP won 47 of the 129 Scottish Parliament seats against 46 for the Labour Party, thus ending the latter's 50 years of political dominance in Scotland. Eighteen parliamentarians short of an absolute majority, the SNP set out to form a minority government which would need support on successive issues from other smaller parties.

A week after the election I finally met with Alex Salmond at Edinburgh's five-star Caledonian Hotel. He had worked out the numbers and equations in the new Parliament and realised that he would need the Greens' two votes, along with other minority votes, to achieve his ambition to be appointed First Minister and be able to form an SNP-led government and get legislation enacted. The Labour Party was clearly going to form the official opposition.

I told the Green Party national council the next day of Salmond's approach. It was agreed that the New Zealand model – in which the minority centre-right National Party governs on the basis of successive *ad hoc* agreements with small parties – was the closest degree of cooperation we could enter into with Salmond and the SNP. This kind of agreement between political parties is known in the trade as a 'confidence and supply' deal. It is less formal than a full-blown coalition but nevertheless allows a substantial minority party to hold power while a yet smaller party, or parties, agree to support the larger party on its budget and on any votes designed by opponents to oust it from power. The 'supply' part of the equation refers to bills required for a minority government to receive money to allow it to enact its policies. 'The 'confidence' part refers to an agreement to give backing on votes of no confidence: it does not allude to the trust, or otherwise, that the signatories to the deal have in each other.[2]

While the SNP badly needed our two votes to get Salmond elected First Minister and to secure its first national budget, politically there was no way we could go into full coalition or too close an alliance.

In a possible deal for our votes, we had our own principles and demands. We agreed to begin negotiating two days after Salmond's approach. We had to use our minimal political power to gain a few important concessions to Green Party ideals. The talks proved intensive and very interesting. We were given a civil servant whose sole task was to assist us with costing any legislation we might secure as part of a bargain.

Three very tough days of negotiations began on the third floor of Old St Andrews House, near the offices of the First Minister of Scotland – who, until Salmond could sort out his and the SNP's problems, was still Labour's Jack McConnell. The SNP delegation was led by John Swinney, designated by Salmond to become Scotland's new Finance Minister, and ours was led by Patrick Harvie since he was covering Swinney's portfolio. Meanwhile, I chaired the Green Party's support and advisory group in an adjoining room.

One consideration for us in the negotiations was that come the fourth Scottish Parliament election, due in May 2011, the arithmetic suggested that a Green seat gained was most likely to be an SNP seat lost, and vice versa. So both sides had a lot to play for. One of our demands, the committee chairmanship of a parliamentary committee, was conceded quite quickly by Swinney. Patrick got the best chairmanship for the Green Party – the committee on climate change, transport and the environment.

* * *

On the second day of negotiations we thought about what we might do if the SNP offered us a ministerial post. Alex Salmond was getting

---

[2] The term 'confidence and supply' originated in 1996 when New Zealand introduced proportional representation for its parliamentary system. Since then confidence and supply agreements have played a key part in negotiations to form successive New Zealand governments.

desperate to form his government. At one point he leant close to me, touched my arm, looked me straight in the eye and, stealing a trick from Tony Blair, said: 'Robin, let's forget all these bits of paper. Just *trust me*.'

It was not something I was inclined to do, and our negotiating team decided that in no circumstances would the Green Party accept a ministry post under Salmond.

On the third day the two sides put together a short memorandum on the outcome of our first round of talks. It came to just a few lines. It provided for us to vote in Parliament for Salmond to become First Minister and for Patrick and me to vote for his SNP government's first national budget. We signed the memo with Alex Salmond and paused to draw breath.

We knew there would be a multitude of TV reporters and their cameras, newspaper journalists and press photographers waiting at Old St Andrews House as we came out on to the entrance steps at the end of the three days of talks. I shared with Patrick and the Green team my concern that any image of a beaming Salmond shaking hands with either Patrick or me would convey a negative and inaccurate image for the Green Party. We were seeking an 'arrangement' with Salmond, not offering him a 'bargain'.

I was photographed looking grim-faced next to Salmond. Anyone who closely knew me understood from my body language that I was not about to embark on any kind of cosy relationship with the SNP. Nevertheless, for months afterwards people asked me questions about the Green 'alliance' with the SNP and, judging from the emails and letters I received, we lost a few members. Even when our 'arrange-ment' with the SNP came to its eventual end some people thought we remained in 'alliance' even though I had lost count of the number of SNP policy proposals we voted against.

A few days later Salmond, now the first Scottish Nationalist to lead Scotland's devolved government thanks to the Green Party's two votes, wanted to release some more details of our arrangement and hold a photo shoot outside Parliament. I reluctantly agreed and took his hand.

* * *

One positive outcome from Patrick Harvie's appointment to chair Parliament's important committee on climate change, transport and the environment was the creation of climate change legislation. Acting with confidence and effectiveness, Patrick steered a Climate Change Bill from the government through his committee and it became law as the Climate Change (Scotland) Act on 4 August 2009. It did not contain anywhere near everything the Green Party wanted, but it is nevertheless the most far-reaching piece of environmental legislation agreed so far by Scotland's Parliament and of course 10 years earlier in the infancy of the Parliament such a day had been beyond our wildest dreams.

Scotland, as a result of the Act, has set itself the world's most ambitious greenhouse gas reduction targets, vowing to cut the nation's carbon emissions by 42 per cent by 2020 and by 80 per cent by 2050. In a rare show of unity, all political parties at Holyrood agreed unanimously to the targets as well as requiring the Scottish government to set legally binding annual cuts in emissions from 2012 onwards. The law was approved a day after the United States said that a 40 per cent cut by 2020 was 'not on the cards': developing nations have demanded this level of cut from rich nations.

The campaign coalition *Stop Climate Chaos Scotland*, which claims its 60 member organisations represent two million people, said this 'hugely significant' vote set a new 'moral' standard for the rest of the industrialised world. Kim Carstensen, head of World Wide Fund for Nature's International's Global Climate Initiative, said: 'At least one nation is prepared to aim for climate legislation that follows the science. Scotland made the first step to show others that it can be done. We now need others to follow.'

Hollywood star and Governor of California Arnold Schwarzenegger applauded the Scottish Parliament move. He said: 'Scotland's ambitious and comprehensive targets encourage other nations to step up to the plate . . . It sends a message to the world that we must act now [on climate change] and we must act swiftly.'

An attempt by Patrick and me to include a 90 per cent target for 2050 – instead of 80 per cent – was rejected. Patrick argued: 'If we are going to include specific targets in this bill, they should be the right targets, not the wrong targets. Those who have studied the subject in detail understand now that 80 per cent is a target which is already out of date.' However, we succeeded in strengthening the Act's provisions to include greenhouse gases emitted by planes and ships in the pollution-reduction targets.

We did succeed in getting the SNP administration to support the Climate Challenge Fund, a key part of our manifesto to enable individuals across Scotland to play their part in reducing carbon emissions by transforming their local environments into Greener places in which to live. It was agreed that £27.4 million would be distributed to community-based projects by the time of the scheduled 2011 election. By June 2010 more than 260 projects had received Climate Challenge Funds, including initiatives to encourage more people to leave their cars at home and use bikes or walk instead; to turn neglected tenement back courts into green and productive gardens; and to make it easier to buy organically produced food. A project in Glasgow, for example, the Shettleston Community Growing Project, received £172,800 for a resident-led initiative to grow food locally and raise awareness of food waste, recycling and energy consumption.

The Fund, perhaps our biggest success because it gets people thinking and acting Green at the all-important local level, gave money to support the Glasgow-based Eco Drama theatre company which tours the country in its Magic Van promoting energy saving, recycling and other eco-friendly, green and healthy ideas. The Magic Van is powered from reclaimed vegetable oil taken from Indian and Chinese takeaway restaurants and fish-and-chip shops! The oil is put through a unique cleaning process before it is poured into the Magic Van – just like mineral diesel, except that it is cheaper, non-toxic and its carbon emissions are 85 per cent lower than in a diesel-run vehicle.

Community groups across the country have set their own agenda and devised their own projects, and it has been truly inspirational to see them putting their ideas into practice, helping the environment, boosting local food and healthier living, cutting energy bills and kickstarting local green jobs. Scotland has become alive with ideas to capture the imagination and make practical differences. I am sure we can claim this as a success for Green Party hopes and ideals. The priority now is to learn from the best projects, and for Parliament to discuss how to build on the successes to benefit more communities in the years to come.

* * *

If the electorate was in any doubt about our independence from the SNP, it evaporated less than two years after the sealing of the SNP-Green Party 'arrangement' when, in January 2009, we plunged the SNP government into turmoil by blocking that year's national budget. With finances shut off, local councils began ringing the government to find out what had happened to the money they needed from the budget: companies were demanding to know if their government contracts were going to be honoured.

The crisis had developed and simmered throughout the summer and autumn of the previous year when Patrick was trying to negotiate with Alex Salmond and John Swinney a programme, based on our manifesto pledge, that would see every home in Scotland insulated to the highest possible standards.[3] This measure of energy conservation would not only keep both poor and rich families warm, it would be the quickest, simplest, cheapest and most effective way of conserving energy and reducing our production of greenhouse gases. It was plain commonsense, a no-brainer, with benefits throughout society, and there was quite a background.

In the course of Scotland's second Parliament global warming had become a big issue for all parties. Nearly everyone began talking about 'greening' the economy, suggesting that investments in renewable energy and energy-saving technologies could both reduce the output of greenhouse gases and create hundreds of thousands of new jobs.

With this change of mood, it was incumbent upon us to propose practical ways of achieving generally agreed goals. One of my obsessions was that if every home in Scotland, a cold country for most of the year, was insulated in roof and walls the saving in energy costs and the

---

[3] See Chapter 14.

reduction in use of fossil fuels would be colossal and make a real contribution to the fight against climate change and increase people's health.

The Green Party said the government should roll out free insulation schemes across the land. Domestic heating consumption would be decreased by 50 to 60 per cent and the struggling construction industry would be given a new lease of life. Half the output of our power stations would be stopped from escaping straight up into the sky.

I argued that any budget allocation for house insulation should be regarded as an investment rather than a cost. I argued passionately that if we did not begin to take this kind of action, allied with others to combat climate change, then within 300 years our planet would probably be uninhabitable. The nature of the challenge is to convince people that there remains time to avert complete catastrophe and that technically we have enough answers. We want Scotland's government to devote £100 million initially to get a free home insulation project off the ground. If all Scottish homes were insulated, our estimate is that the average household could save nearly £350 a year, a total saving of nearly a billion pounds annually. In addition, our annual carbon emissions would be cut by six per cent.

Be bold, we argue in Parliament, and such home energy efficiency will prove to be the most cost-effective way to beat fuel poverty, improve health, tackle climate change and cut people's bills all at the same time.

We constantly quote a real example of practical success. The Kirklees Council, in the Yorkshire Pennine Hills of northern England, cut the Huddersfield area's annual carbon emissions by 28,000 tonnes after it offered all its residents free cavity-wall and loft insulation, with energy-saving light bulbs and a £40 carbon monoxide detector thrown in. The Kirklees Warm Zone initiative, funded with £20 million for its first three years, grew into Britain's biggest council-run home insulation programme. Free insulation work was carried out on more than 100,000 homes, leading to an average household reduction of £200 on annual fuel bills, a total yearly saving of £6.5 million for the Huddersfield area population. More than 100 jobs were created implementing the scheme before it came to an end in June 2010. At the Warm Zone's height, 600 free energy-saving installations were being carried out each week.

Surely, I and my fellow Green parliamentarians argue, if a council in a poor area of England can do it, then the powerful Scottish government can emulate it.

The evidence of the success of the Kirklees scheme was there for all to hear from the local residents. Pauline Pedley, a 72-year-old retired teacher from the village of Mirfield, near Huddersfield, said she first heard of Warm Zone when a leaflet dropped through her door. She said she was 'shocked that it was free', but applied. Within two weeks her house had been surveyed and her loft was insulated and the cavity walls pumped with insulation material in just a day. 'It made such a difference,' said Mrs Pedley. 'With the insulation and my double-glazing, I rarely have to have the heating on. The free help is particularly good for pensioners like me who couldn't afford it otherwise.'

John Rowden, 65, a retired sales manager living with his wife, Pat, 63, in a detached four-bedroom house in Batley, seven miles from Huddersfield, said his free loft insulation was ten inches thick. 'You can feel such a big difference,' said Mr Rowden. 'Physically, you could tell it was working because it was noticeably hotter in the summer and obviously better in winter. It took a matter of hours and you couldn't fault the work.' Mr Rowden credited Warm Zone with 'helping me realise the importance of energy efficiency in my own life. This isn't just about saving money but about the future of the planet, what we are going to leave for our grandchildren. The scheme should be run nationwide.'

Warm Zone enjoys cross-party support in Kirklees. Labour Party leader Mehboob Khan said: 'Our residents couldn't believe the council was going to give them free insulation. They thought it must be a con trick.' But homes were soon signing up in droves. 'We're tackling fuel poverty and reducing carbon emissions. For every £1 we spend, local people save £4 on their fuel bills. There's no reason why other councils can't run similar schemes. There are far more affluent councils than Kirklees, some of them sitting on capital reserves running into hundreds of millions of pounds. Where there's a will, there's always a way.'[4]

Unfortunately, the will was weak in Alex Salmond's ruling Scottish National Party government. For whatever perverse reasons, the SNP administration dillied and dallied with our home insulation proposals that would have made all Scotland's homes warmer. In response to our request for £100 million a year for 10 years to provide insulation for the nation's near-two million homes, the SNP initially offered a derisory £2 million to get the programme started. Set against a target set by the Salmond administration to cut carbon dioxide emissions by at least 42 per cent by 2025, this would be less effective than spitting on a hot iron.

Patrick Harvie quite rightly rejected this and for months Alex Salmond and John Swinney ignored us until, in January 2009, with just a few hours to go before the 2009 budget was due to be voted on by Parliament, Salmond came up with £33 million a year, far short of the £100 million we considered necessary for a fully successful programme. We were, however, willing to compromise but first wanted to see whether it was real new money or fantasy money taken from other important projects. We were particularly concerned that the money being offered might be stolen from the 'fuel poverty' allocation, allowances to the very poor and elderly as subsidies for their bills so that they could keep warm through the long winter.

Because we had supported the 2008 budget as part of the SNP/Green Party 'arrangement', the SNP had taken for granted our likely support for the new budget. Now they were unable to give us an assurance that the poor would not be robbed to fulfill their promise to us, and, despite their last minute panic offer of additional money, they had allowed us no time to consult our party members. So we voted against the budget and it fell.

Few people would have predicted that a parliamentary budget anywhere in the world would fall on the issue of loft insulation, but energy-efficiency remains to this day the best climate change legislation Scotland has never had!

[4] *The Times*, 12 October 2009, 'Kirklees cuts carbon emissions with its free installation scheme'; Roger Harrabin, BBC environmental analyst, 11 June 2009.

Alex Salmond almost burst a blood vessel with anger. 'Were he [Salmond] an ape, I'd have been calling for the fences to be electrified in his compound lest he escape and start running amok among the general populace,' wrote Rab McNeil, parliamentary sketch writer of *The Scotsman*. 'I've never seen him so enraged. If you'd put a pie on his head, it would have been piping hot in two minutes.'

The roof did not fall in. The SNP came back a few weeks later having made little bribes to all the other parties – who accepted them – and reduced its energy conservation targets to a bare minimum, with the money allocated to home insulation back down to the original offer of £2 million.

At the end of the day, we had learned a lot about the exercise of real power, however limited it had been, and we may use the SNP betrayal on home insulation to make it a big issue in the 2011 and fourth Parliamentary election. We continue to campaign for 'Warm Scotland', with a logo showing a house wrapped in my Dr Who rainbow-coloured scarf! We will win on this issue in the long run, and we are confident we will take seats from the SNP and that a new government will introduce secure, wise and effective home insulation legislation.

19

Trees

The great Scottish naturalist John Muir, whose campaigns led to the establishment of the Yosemite and Sequoia National Parks in the United States and who devoted the latter part of his life to saving the great forests of the American West, said any fool could destroy trees.[1]

I share Muir's passion for trees, and have reared hundreds of them from seed and planted them in many parts of Scotland, sometimes in my schoolmaster role, sometimes as a politician, and often just in my own personal right.

Trees are our planet's lungs, absorbing carbon and modifying suffocating greenhouse gas emissions, providing homes for wild creatures and just standing there being beautiful. Their roots secure river banks and slow increasingly destructive and disastrous rain run-offs. They can even, if harvested sensibly, provide a sustainable supply of eco-friendly fuel.

Scotland is a picturesque country, but surprisingly few people realise that its heather-coated mountains and hills were once clothed in great forests. As a result of the industrial revolution, during which woodland was annihilated in swathes for building materials and fuel, and of heavy over-grazing by sheep and deer, more than 90 per cent of the country's forests were wiped out. Millennia of deforestation mean that only small remnants and single solitary trees are all that remain of these once noble forests.

Nothing is quite as symbolic of Scotland's lost wilderness as the sad old remnants of the Great Forest of Caledon. The Great Forest,

---

[1] Muir's quote in full reads: 'God has cared for these trees, saved them from drought, disease, avalanches, and a thousand tempests and floods. But he cannot save them from fools.'

dominated by magnificent stands of Scots pine and aspen, once covered nearly 6,000 square miles of the Scottish Highlands. Today the Great Forest of Caledon is reduced to barely 65 square miles, in scattered stands, mainly consisting of trees more than 150 years old, moribund and in terminal decay, their saplings relentlessly munched, before they can regenerate, by unacceptably high populations of sheep and red deer. These grazers and browsers have no natural predators to control their numbers because, along with the disappearance of the trees of the Great Forest, so have its magnificent hunting animals, lynx, wolf and brown bear, also been wiped out.

In Scotland's southern Border hills, naturalists estimate that 99 per cent of the original woodland has been destroyed, leaving bare, sheep-covered hills that are effectively grass deserts. With growing awareness of the sins of the past, various initiatives have arisen in efforts to reverse the decline of our woodlands and wild places. I gave £250 in 2000 when a group of about 600 people got together to recreate four square miles of lost forest in a barren glen in the Border hills that was devoid of trees and wildlife.

Now, thanks to donations totalling many hundreds of thousands of pounds, the valley of the Carrifran River, rising at more than 2,600 feet, has been bought from its previous owner and planted with some half a million trees. The kind of lush, deciduous woodland that clothed the Carrifran valley 6,000 years ago is gradually being restored. Oak, alder, juniper, aspen, bird cherry, wych elm, rowan, ash, birch and several species of willow are reclaiming ancient haunts. Wildlife is returning – otters, peregrine falcons, skylarks, kestrels, ravens, reed buntings, willow warblers, buzzards, black grouse. Golden eagles and ospreys have been sighted. It is a fantastic example of how it is possible to take a piece of devastated hill land and over a relatively short period restore it to ecological health.

As a trustee of the Carrifran Wildwood project, I planted 23 oak, rowan, alder and birch saplings in the Carrifran valley to offset my air miles, adding to global pollution, accumulated when I flew in 2002 to Johannesburg to attend the United Nations' World Summit on Sustainable Development, the so-called Earth Summit.

The first Carrifran saplings were planted by volunteers in January

140

2000. Scientists have identified the trees that grew in the original Carrifran wild forest from a complete pollen record taken from peat bogs on the site. Some of the trees planted in 2000 are now more than six metres high: those that fall over are left to decay or regrow. The old adage about mighty oaks from little acorns is unavoidable. Elsewhere, a furring of young saplings is spreading along the valley sides. Dr Philip Ashmole, a retired zoologist and one of the Carrifran pioneers, said:

> We set up the Wildwood project to show that, in a world weighed down with environmental problems, we don't have to just sit back and wring our hands. We can take action and do something positive. This project proves that people have the power to reverse environmental harm, and we hope it will inspire others to come up with even bolder schemes to restore areas that have been degraded down the centuries.

Dr Ashmole has described how he had a 'Road to Damascus' experience while walking across the Scottish Border hills in the mid-1990s. Mile after mile of windblown grasslands rolled like ocean waves before him. What he was seeing filled him with a profound sense of loss. There was nothing but grass, grass and yet more grass, an almost naked landscape, the dismal result of thousands of years of over-grazing by sheep and feral goats. 'Then I looked out over the glistening waters of Loch Skene [a trout-rich lake high amidst treeless hills near Carrifran] and there, in the middle of the loch, was a tiny island,' said Dr Ashmole. 'I peered through my binoculars and on that wee island I saw a solitary birch tree. I threw up my hands. "Oh my God," I said, "there ought to be trees all round here." I realised the tree had survived only because the wretched sheep and goats couldn't get to it.'[2]

It dawned on Dr Ashmole that a group of local activists should get together, buy a denuded landscape and restore its original woodland instead of just talking endlessly and wringing hands.

[2] *SCOTS Magazine*. 'Carrifran Wildwood,' by Dr Philip Ashmole, 26 May 2009.

If you look at a satellite photograph of Scotland you see across its wild lands an extraordinary lack of forest, except for deadening commercial single-species conifer plantations, mainly of sitka spruce, a fast-growing North American import, planted in militarily disciplined rows upon rows. While teaching at Boroughmuir High School I used to help with residential summer holiday expeditions for the entire second year at the Lochgoilhead National Activity Centre in the Western Highlands. The kids sailed, rock-climbed and walked in the mountains. One year I took a group of more than 20 on a 'tree walk', showing them different native trees while railing against the ugly sitka spruce plantations. Crossing one cleared slope, a boy pointed up the hillside and said: 'Sir, see up there, that tree that man's planting, what is it?' I look up and he was clearly planting the dreaded tree. 'Sitka spruce,' I replied. The boy's brow furrowed and he exclaimed, 'Sir, shall I go up and tell him off?' I counselled against it.

The Carrifran example is being emulated elsewhere. The need for reforestation was emphasised when hundreds of delegates from around the globe gathered in Edinburgh in July 2010 to discuss worldwide programmes for forest restoration and protection. James Rollinson, head of the Forestry Commission, the government department responsible for the protection and expansion of Britain's forests and woodlands, told delegates that forests lock up carbon and help to regulate the climate, so we need them to help keep the Earth's climate in balance – 'In short, without forests we're in serious trouble, and yet they are still being lost and degraded at an alarming rate.'

The Woodland Trust in Scotland, which seeks to restore Scotland's lost forests and woods, argues that 24 square miles should be planted with new trees each year for the next 50 years in order to restore a truly healthy forest cover. Scotland's government has set a target of planting 100 million new trees by 2015.

One hundred years ago only five per cent of Scotland's land area was clothed in trees, making us one of the least wooded countries in Europe. Visitors to Scotland who marvel at the wild beauty of our Highland hills and rocky islands need to know that what they are in fact seeing is a moonscape, an example of widespread devastation by industrialised man and his grazing beasts.

I can trace my own concern with trees back to my time teaching in western Kenya where I was struck by the beauty of its and neighbouring Uganda's tropical forests and, in the high mountains, the temperate forests. By that time, in the late 1960s and early 1970s, science had established that healthy forests played an absolutely critical role in regulating the world's climate and temperatures. Next to curbing mankind's wanton burning of fossil fuels, we need as a matter of great urgency a worldwide plan to conserve these carbon stores together with plans to restore forest growth, particularly in the Himalayas, Oceania and tropical Africa and South America. Massive floods in Mozambique in 2000 and in Pakistan in 2010 were largely the result of deforestation in the headwaters of the Zambezi and Limpopo Rivers in the case of Mozambique, and in the mountain and plains stretches of the mighty 2,000-mile-long Indus River in Pakistan.

'The watersheds of the rivers flowing into Mozambique are so drastically impaired by man they are no longer able to absorb heavy rainfall and discharge it slowly into river beds over the course of a year,' according to Dr Janet Abramovitz, a senior researcher at the Worldwatch Institute in Washington DC. 'The Limpopo watershed, for example, has lost 99 per cent of its original forest cover. In river after river we see that the result is extreme floods and extreme droughts. When you factor in climatic change, the unfortunate truth is the land is less and less able to deal with violent weather storms. What we have is a frightening scenario.'

This was mirrored in Pakistan where trees felled by so-called illegal loggers – an infamous 'timber mafia' which has representatives in the Pakistan Parliament in Islamabad and connections right to the top of government and the military – were stacked in the innumerable nullahs (steep narrow valleys), gorges and ravines leading into the main rivers. From there they were fed into the legal trade, earning the mafia billions of dollars yearly. But the deforestation was a ticking time-bomb waiting for a trigger to set off explosions. The 2010 monsoon lashing northern Pakistan with unusual intensity would in the past have been absorbed by extensive forests, much like multiple layers of blotting paper, allowing the rains to run off more sedately than in recent times. But the mud and water deluge cascaded off tree-bare mountains and hills with exceptional force and barrelled down towards the plains in mammoth fury. Propelled by the force of the run-off, the masses of stacked illegal timber turned into instruments of destruction, smashing all in their wake. Rivers and dams turned black with tree trunks. Relief workers said bridges, homes and people were destroyed and swept away by the hurtling and swirling logs before the waters spread onto the plains below, engulfing an area of more than 60,000 square miles, more than twice the land area of Scotland.[3]

All this means that we have to see world poverty, which is a major concern of the Green Party, as both an environmental problem and a human problem. Abject poverty is environmentally corrosive: in the absence of wise control or guidance by governments, expanding populations of impoverished peoples are inevitably reduced to chopping down trees for fuel or for extra land for cultivation. Solutions to widespread destitution almost defy answer, but I believe the Big Powers and the United Nations will have to cooperate and buy huge areas of the world's forests, particularly in the Congo and Amazon Basins and the East Indian islands, to ensure their permanent conservation while at the same time somehow ensuring a stable economic future for the people who live within or near them.

---

[3] 'Disaster is just the beginning,' *Sunday Herald*, 5 March 2000; 'A land left to drown by the "timber mafia",' *Sunday Herald*, 29 August 2010.

20

I discover I have an additional brother

In 1989, as I approached my 50th birthday, I was hit with a bombshell revelation about my family's history.

I had been invited to visit my parents at their retirement cottage in Walberton, a prim and pretty little village near Arundel in West Sussex. I was feeling high as I travelled the 500 miles southwards from Scotland. I had just achieved a stunningly good result in a European Parliament election. In an electoral 'first' nationally for the Green Party, fighting for an Edinburgh seat, I had broken the 10 per cent-of-the-total-vote barrier – unfortunately, far from enough to get me elected to the Brussels and Strasbourg-based Parliament, but a breakthrough nonetheless in Green historic terms.

In Walberton I detected immediately in Pa an unusually high level of excitement and a kind of nervous distraction and agitation in Mum's demeanour. They ushered me into their tiny and snug living room, lined with books and paintings and photographs of the ships on which Pa had served. Almost in chorus, they said: 'We think you should sit down. We've got something to tell you.'

They said that Mum was in a state of shock following an approach by a lawyer on behalf of someone I would not have known of – her *real* first son. Mum had had an affair with another man before she married Pa, and became pregnant. The baby had been given away for adoption.

They let this bolt from the blue sink in, and Pa then asked: 'Do you think Mum should agree to meet him [her long lost son]?'

At this point we as a family had close to zero information about this very close relative. He could have been anything from a priest or professor to a despot or drunkard, but nevertheless my instant reply was: Yes, yes, you must meet him.

Bit by bit, I put the story together, although I am unsure to this day that I have got it all completely right.

My mum, as a young and beautiful Jessica Pinfold, just 24 years old, met my Pa, Peter Harper, at a party in Buckinghamshire in 1935. Pa was attracted to her and invited her for tea aboard his ship, the battlecruiser HMS *Renown*, in Portsmouth. Fate intervened and he sailed with his ship at a day's notice to the Mediterranean in a vain attempt to deter Italy from invading Ethiopia. On return, Peter met Jessica a few times before sailing to Hong Kong, where he was Secretary to the Commodore at the land base HMS *Tamar* until 1939. Peter was obviously deeply smitten by Jessica because for the next two and a half years he plied her with letters from China, where, in addition to his naval service, he hosted a children's pro-gramme for Hong Kong Radio. He also saw his mother and father in Tientsin for the last time before they were interned in a prison camp by the Japanese for the duration of the Second World War. He did not see them again for another 10 years until after the war in Britain.

Jessica, in Peter's absence, was working in central London as a secretary at the Institute for Historical Research where she had an affair with one of the researchers. When she became pregnant her family in Gillingham threw her out of the house and refused to support her. Jessica's mother had died when she was young and my mother told me in the final years of her life that she believed her stepmother, whom she disliked, was behind this rather than her father, George. Jessica gave birth to a son in Gravesend, near her home town, on 3 November 1936.

I had always been puzzled, while growing up, by the attentions of a group of three non-family 'aunties', close friends of my mother scarcely separable from my real aunts. These 'aunties' regularly sent Euan and me birthday and Christmas presents and cards and occa-sionally paid us visits. They had worked in the same City of London typing pool as Mum in the 1930s and they had all clearly developed deep loyalties towards each other. One of them became my godmother and left me her family silver when she died.

These saintly 'aunties', I learned, found Jessica lodgings in London and supported her from their typists' small wages throughout her pregnancy. Mum realised fairly quickly that she would be unable to support her baby on her own and accepted the painful truth that she would need to endure the heartbreak of giving him up for adoption.

The whole drama surrounding illegitimate births and the administration of adoption in the 1930s was a cruel one. All adoptions then were conducted in strict secrecy on the absolute understanding that there would be no further contact between mother and child. All parental and legal rights of the mother were severed and transferred to the new adoptive family. All identifying information relating to the biological parent was sealed and made secret, forbidding by law any disclosure of the child's true parenthood.

'The lot of the unmarried mother was a very unhappy one,' wrote Sue Elliott, herself given up as a baby for adoption, in a perceptive article in *The Times*.

> Unlike our secular society today, religion – a rather puritan form of Protestantism – permeated public and private life and determined social policy. Marriage was the only acceptable basis for family life and a cruel double standard operated against women when it came to sexual behaviour: men couldn't help themselves, but women were responsible for the purity of the home and the bloodline.
>
> But I can see now how it happened. Britain was in the economic doldrums . . . The welfare state didn't exist and inflexible moral attitudes prescribed a very narrow range of choices for unmarried mothers. Birth parents were considered the least important participants in the adoption triangle and many suffered inhumane treatment that caused a lifetime's unhappiness and sometimes worse.[1]

Reunion was certainly not part of the plan. Legal adoptions, including that of my mother's child, were conducted on the absolute understanding that there would be no further contact between mother and child – ever. The laws surrounding adoption cut off Jessica from the

---

[1] 'Adoption: a cruel and desperate system', by Sue Elliott, *The Times* of London, 5 January 2005.

possibility of knowing what happened to her child, and for her child it removed a crucial part of his identity jigsaw.

The man who made Mum pregnant fell seriously ill that same year and refused to take any responsibility. Ironically, in view of my subsequent relationship with the city and its education institutions, he fled north to Aberdeen where he took a lecturing job and faded from view, although my family has since learned he died some time around 1980.

David was adopted by a remarkable unmarried lady in Northern Ireland who had independent income and who was so interested in children that she had also adopted two others. By David's account, she was a good mother and a woman of considerable character and intelligence. David, of course, took her surname, Roulston. During the Second World War they lived on the Northern Ireland coast, moving to Bangor – 14 miles from Belfast, the capital – after the war.

David flourished at the local grammar school and then graduated with an electronics degree from Queen's University, Belfast, subsequently completing a Ph.D in electronic engineering at Imperial College, London.

Dr David Roulston married a French woman and they worked together in France for many years, having three children. Differences between them eventually led to their separation and divorce. David kept the children and raised them himself in Canada, where he began a 30-year teaching career at Waterloo University in Ontario Province while researching the engineering physics of microchips. For the final 10 years of his career he carried out research at Oxford University and settled nearby.

When his adoptive mother died he decided to try to trace his biological mother. It took him a few years. A change in British law in 1975 made this possible. The reform permitted adoptees the right, for the first time, to be given access to their original birth records. His research led him, during a visit to London, to the adoption society Jessica had chosen. There he read letters she had written to the society both before and after his birth: her obvious concern for her infant's happiness and well-being inspired him to press on. Searching records at St Catherine's House in central London, where public records were

148

held until 1997, he found Jessica's birth certificate and what looked like the recording of her marriage to a Lieutenant-Commander C.H.A. Harper in 1939.

On return to Canada, he hired a solicitor in England who advised him to contact the Navy wing of Britain's Defence Ministry and ask for help in contacting Jessica and Lieutenant-Commander Harper. The ministry gave David my parents' address and he wrote to Jessica who, while overjoyed at hearing from her lost son, was nervous and reticent about a possible meeting. A few months passed before David received another letter from Pa saying that while Mum was 'slightly paranoid' about telling Euan and me about the existence of her 'other son', he was sure that once she had plucked up the courage to break the news we would both be delighted to meet David. Pa was right on that score.

Mum met David again in a hotel in central London for the first time since he was he was taken away from her 53 years earlier. David told me that their conversation was initially slightly strained, but they both relaxed and laughed after she burst out: 'I am so glad you don't sound like Ian Paisley [the fiery Northern Ireland politician and Protestant church minister].' She derived great happiness in the three years she had with her son until she died from a stroke in 1992. Euan and I met him for the first time when he visited Mum, Pa, Euan and me together in Edinburgh.

David, it turned out, shared many of our family interests in music, literature, art and history and my own particular concerns about the environment and conservation. Happiness is the only word that spells the consequences of his entry into our lives. We love him to bits and are as close as the best of brothers should be. David now lives in retirement at Bladon, in Oxfordshire, near Winston Churchill's last resting place in the graveyard of St Martin's Church, where David and his second wife, Rosalyn, were married. We visit each other frequently and I particularly enjoy sailing with David on his beloved boat *Dabchick*.

Pa was chuffed to bits that David had rediscovered his biological mother and right up until Pa died in 2003 he treated David as his own son, travelling with him to various places, including Paris, Vienna and

Salzburg. David was able to share wide interests with Mum and Pa in music, poetry and literature. Mum was especially delighted to discover that her granddaughter, David's daughter Christine, had become a Professor of English and French Literature in Canada and shared Jessica's love of the poetry of William Wordsworth.

21

My family life is completed

I was invited at short notice by a journalist friend of mine, Caroline Dempster, to entertain guests at a New Year party at the beginning of 1990. I hurriedly selected a red sweater, pulled on a jacket, tucked my guitar under my arm and turned up at the large flat where the bash was being held.

Spying three large holes in the front of my sweater, Caroline persuaded me to reverse it under my jacket. 'You have to look reasonably presentable, Robin,' she said. 'After all, you might meet the woman of your dreams.'

How right she was.

As I performed, a pretty woman with a bright smile caught my eye. I later talked to her and offered to see her home. This proved remarkably easy, as she lived in the flat opposite on the same landing. Her name was Jenny Carter, a divorcee with an 11-year-old son. Having seen her home, I took a taxi back to my own flat feeling distinctly that something good and significant had begun in my life. We exchanged a few phone calls, went on a date and I do not recall a day since then when we have not been in touch with each other in one way or the other.

One Sunday in June 1993, we together climbed Arthur's Seat, an 823-feet-high volcanic hill which provides a highland landscape in the centre of Edinburgh, where I proposed to her. She said yes, and it was a wonderful feeling descending the hill holding hands and knowing a new and wonderful chapter of my life had begun.

I was very busy with politics and the Green Party by this time and attending evening and Saturday courses as a teacher to improve my Guidance skills. Jenny was a full-time businesswoman, running her own corporate communications agency as well as beginning a Masters degree. They were very good, busy and productive days for both of us. We found, happily, that we shared many other interests, including music, theatre, the arts, walking and a love of mainland Europe, in particular France.

I am so lucky to have found Jenny as a partner. She has been incredibly supportive of what to her must have seemed my rather quixotic approach to politics. She never grumbled about the amount of time I gave to what must have appeared to be either a hopeless cause or, at best, a long-term struggle. Although she has never become a party member, she designed the 1999 Green Party manifesto and she has joined me in the unavoidable but necessary leafleting and postering at election time. She keeps me connected with the real world out there beyond the bubble of party politics.

We married in September 1994. I wanted a church wedding, but when I asked my friend Canon Bill Brockie if he would perform the ceremony he reminded me that I would need the permission of the Episcopalian Bishop of Edinburgh to marry a divorcee. I was surprised that the Episcopal Church still insisted on this formality, but the Bishop, the very liberal Richard Holloway, gave us his blessing.

Our wedding was very Green. Clutching the orders of service, I simply caught a number 11 bus to Christ Church in the Edinburgh suburb of Bruntsfield, where I was joined by Jenny who was given a car lift to the church by Caroline Dempster, who had brought us together. There followed a wedding lunch in the home of close friends Mike and Therese Duriez; a huge *ceilidh* in the Assembly Rooms in central Edinburgh; a honeymoon night in a suite in Niddrie Castle, where Mary Queen of Scots was given shelter after her escape from captivity in 1568; and an extended honeymoon on the island of Jersey.

Our married life changed after my election to Parliament in 1999. We were both busy before that date, but life turned frenetic after it. Jenny learned how to manage and coordinate our personal diaries by speaking to Alison Johnston, my personal assistant in Parliament for the first eight years, and Sally Cowburn latterly. One of my challenges was getting used to being managed by more than one woman.

The sheer pressure of work meant that it became harder and harder to keep up with friends. As the political rollercoaster gathered speed, Jenny was my anchor through its many ups and downs. She sometimes typed my speeches late at night and was always willing to listen to the excitements – or disappointments – of my day. She was endlessly patient as media people interrupted for cellphone interviews even on our snatched holidays.

There were many positives to my new life as a parliamentarian that we were able to enjoy together – the exhilarating day of the opening of the first Scottish Parliament on 1 July 1999, for example, and many other events to which I was invited as a party leader. I can be quite stubborn and it took me time to discover how much Jenny worked covertly with my team to ensure that my general health and welfare were taken care of. Down time was inserted into my overflowing diary; health checks were organized; and I was forced to be realistic about limits to my energy levels.

Having a stepson in my life has brought me immense pleasure. I lived with Roy through his teenage years and saw him grow into a bright, capable and charming young man. Much to my amusement he chose my alma mater, Aberdeen, for his university career and even became editor of the student newspaper *Gaudie*, to which I had contributed columns many decades before. In 1995 I was a proud stepdad at his wedding to his delightful wife, Sarah.

Aged 54, before I married Jenny, my known surviving family had consisted only of me and my brother Euan. It seems nothing short of miraculous that these days I have also a second brother, a wife, son and daughter-in-law of my own to share my life with. As I ease out of the Parliament, I look forward to spending more time and new adventures with all of them.

22

My music

Music has been a fundamental pleasure throughout most of my life, a huge part of my hinterland both as a performer and listener.

Both my parents were accomplished pianists. My father began learning to play the piano when he was just four years old and throughout his life he played for spells as a professional church organist, including the period after he retired to Sussex and played at St Mary's Parish Church, Walberton, until he died at the age of 92.

Mozart was Pa's passion, and he used to tick off the Köchel catalogue number for every new performance he heard on the radio of one of the great composer's more than 600 works, written in a remarkably short period of time before his death at the age of 36.[1] By the time of Pa's death, there were hardly any of Mozart's compositions he had not heard.

Pa was also a great fan of Johann Sebastian Bach, but he played piano across a wide repertoire and gave spirited renditions at parties of the wickedly witty satirical songs of Tom Lehrer and those of the jazz genius Fats Waller.

I only began learning the piano when I was aged 11, which is too late if you ever hope to be a virtuoso. Within a couple of years I was entered into a piano competition at a London music festival. It was a horrific experience. I gave a brisk performance of a Bach prelude, but then my fingers turned to jelly as I was obliged to rattle off a series of

---

[1] The 551-page Köchel document is a complete chronological catalogue of compositions by Wolfgang Amadeus Mozart (1756–91) originally created by Ludwig von Köchel. For example, Mozart's *Requiem in D minor* was, according to Köchel's counting, the 626th and final piece Mozart composed.

scales. I stumbled off the stage in embarrassment and asked Mum to stop sending me to piano lessons. It could have – but did not! – put me off performing in public for ever.

I continued to learn to play violin and clarinet at school and the bugle with the Sea Cadet Corps. And I can still play some of the Bach, Schumann and Mozart piano pieces I learned all those years ago.

It was in my second year at Aberdeen University that I began to learn how to play the guitar, through an interest in folk music I shared with several friends. Peter Booth taught me to play a few chords on his treasured guitar, with a soft and sweet sound quality, made by Vicente Tatay of Valencia, one of the great classical guitar makers. Peter eventually gave me his Tatay when he began to concentrate on steel-strung guitar and American folk and blues.

Learning to play the guitar was by a long way one of the most difficult tasks I have attempted. But I so fell in love with the instrument that I practised hard, often between lectures, and became quite an accomplished player. I began giving guitar lessons on Saturday mornings in exchange for breakfast and a copy of the morning newspaper, and for decades afterwards I taught young and old alike in what I like to think was a painless way – thanks to the patient tuition I had been given by Peter.

I also founded the Aberdeen University Folk Club; performed regularly at the city Folk Club; and helped Archie Fisher, one of Scotland's leading folk singers and a master guitarist, run the Elbow Room Folk Club in Kirkcaldy when I began working from 1964 onwards at Braehead School. I also performed at the Elbow Room, sometimes as the main act.

* * *

It was in 1965 that I sang way down the bill one night at Chalk Farm Folk Club in London with a young Martin Carthy, one of the most influential figures in British traditional music, as the star turn. A 24-year-old American singer, earning about £20 a week playing around British folk clubs, was also on the bill. He impressed me and I went with him the next day to Martin's home in north London. I sang for him a version of the traditional ballad 'Scarborough Fair', whose roots in British song can be traced back to 1670 and maybe even further. It's the song whose main verse goes:

> Are you going to Scarborough Fair?
> Parsley, sage, rosemary and thyme,
> Remember me to one who lives there,
> She once was a true love of mine.

'Scarborough Fair' was also in Martin's repertoire. The American's name was Paul Simon. He had never before heard 'Scarborough Fair', but within two years he and Art Garfunkel, a fellow New Yorker, had recorded it as part of the soundtrack of *The Graduate*, one of the highest-grossing Hollywood movies ever. The film helped make 'Scarborough Fair' perhaps the most widely heard folk song of all time, selling millions on various chart-topping discs released by the duo.

I thought of inviting the then-unknown Paul Simon to the Elbow Room but never got round to it. Martin Carthy alleged that Simon and Garfunkel's famous version of the song was adapted from his own special arrangement without acknowledgement: some kind of legal settlement was made in 1970 and in 2000 Martin and Paul Simon sang 'Scarborough Fair' together in concert for the first time. 'Scarborough Fair' remains in my own repertoire, but my role in the rise and rise of Simon and Garfunkel and the runaway success of the song has somehow faded into obscurity and the mists of time . . .

*   *   *

In 1972 I formed with three other musicians what became known as Scotland's only baroque folk band. In our own small way, we were very successful. Fourth Estaite played a variety of club, hotel and pub gigs and at festivals in Edinburgh, York and Leicester. At York, where our mandate was to busk and provide fun on the streets, the crowd once booed an over-officious policeman who had tried to move us on. We provided music backing for plays at the Edinburgh Festival and Edinburgh's Lyceum Theatre.

In striped blazer and tight trousers I was Fourth Estaite's lead singer and guitarist and virtually everything else – driver, semi-manager, scene shifter, accountant. John Sampson played trumpet and various mediaeval instruments: he was in fact a musical genius, able to get tunes out of any instrument that could be blown, from tiny in size to enormous. Rab Handleigh was a very gifted violinist, and Dave Murricane played double bass. Our self-management was pretty chaotic and we never rehearsed formally. Travelling to gigs, we would arrange ourselves in my Renault 4 around Dave's double bass and sing together while Rab's violin bow zipped in and out of a car window.

We performed for the best part of a decade. For most of our career, the Fourth Estaite team got on extremely well. We never played a rigid programme, apart from agreeing the first number in each set, with me calling the numbers as we went along. It kept us on our toes and meant that we never gave the same performance twice. We sang three- and four-part harmonies and our repertoire included Greek, Jewish, Russian music and anything zippy, indeed an eclectic mix of everything from funky to classical.

It was all huge fun. However, John and Rab had different approaches to music. John was given – and remains so – to wild extemporary demonstrations of extraordinary dexterity and skill. Rab could be a classical harmonist in everything he did: in performances of the jazz standard 'Sweet Georgia Brown' I have heard him insert snippets from at least three classical violin concertos.

John and Rab could, at times, differ violently on music matters and I had to step in to prevent them coming to blows on two occasions. Once it was in the middle of a public performance, when John's over-exuberance wrecked one of Rab's beautifully constructed harmonies. 'You fucking bastard, you played a sixth,' roared Rab as he advanced towards John, intent on physical assault, before I managed to get between them.

We got work by word of mouth, made a recording and considered turning full-time professional. We eventually went our separate ways but still get together on special occasions to perform for friends and relatives. When Jenny and I got married on 24 September 1994 John played a Trumpet Voluntary as we smiled our way down the aisle and John and Rab together entertained our guests with a frenetic version of *The Faery Dance* and other Scottish tunes as we had our photographs taken outside the church.

John is these days Scotland's best known theatre musician, a multi-instrument entertainer and director who tours with top entertainers, including Britain's Glasgow-born poet laureate Carol Ann Duffy, in poetry and music recitals. In one virtuoso piece that has become renowned, 'Schizophrenia', John plays two recorders and hums at the same time! Rab is music director at Hereford's highly successful Courtyard Theatre complex and Centre for the Arts. Dave conducts and composes for several performers and runs his own music post-production recording facility in Glasgow. I, of course, am now a veteran professional politician.

* * *

While teaching at Boroughmuir and playing with Fourth Estaite, I also taught for 20 years at the week-long annual summer Dankworth Music Camps in the extensive grounds of the lovely Old Rectory home of jazz singer Cleo Laine and her husband the late Sir John Dankworth, one of the totemic figures of British jazz.

John's younger sister Avril, an accomplished pianist and music lecturer, thought an annual music camp would be the ideal way to give young people two of her main loves – camping and music. Cleo and John allowed her to use two fields behind their house in Wavendon, Buckinghamshire, and also The Stables, the modern 400-seat theatre-cum-arts centre they had built in old stables at the bottom of their garden. Avril specified that the musical experience should be completely different to what the campers experienced at school. It should embrace all fashions, all abilities and should take place as much as possible outdoors.

I met Avril in 1972, two years after she had held her first Music Camp, when she visited Edinburgh to see our innovative work at the Theatre Workshop. Over lunch she described to me the ethos of the camps, a combination of sheer enjoyment of music for its own sake and a liberation from formalities that comes with living in the open air, which I immediately found entrancing. Avril, courtesy of Cleo and John, provided opportunities for youngsters to get involved in all manner of activities they had never tried before. There was instruction in string, brass, steel drums and bell ringing. Full orchestras and jazz bands were formed. In the same band you could find both the Welsh Young Musician of the Year and a disabled boy who could play only five notes on a recorder but who was full of joy at being included.

I offered my services to Avril on the spot as a guitar teacher, and towards the end of my two decades became the camp director and producer of the operetta, attended by parents, that the kids performed in The Stables at the end of the week. Mostly we performed works that had already been written for young people, but on one occasion the kids and staff wrote, produced and performed our own operetta all in the space of seven days.

The camps usually took place while John and Cleo were touring in the United States, but I recall on one occasion John playing double bass while the kids sang with Cleo around the camp fire. At other times, Cleo read stories to the children while the Dankworths' daughter Jacqui took part in one of our operettas.

If only all music education was like that at Avril's camps!

* * *

My music career began to go on hold when I became a parliamentarian. But in 1999 I put together a show, with some of the more musically adept Members of the Scottish Parliament, to raise funds for the charity ChildLine, a Britain-wide counselling service for children and young people, and to celebrate the opening of the first modern-era Scottish Parliament. Arranging this was a task harder than herding cats, but all gave good accounts of themselves on the night. It inspired me to perform and produce a show, Robin Harper and Friends, at the Edinburgh Festival Fringe for the following 10 years, again on behalf of ChildLine. Jenny said I managed each year to spring a song on her she had never heard before. I still love performing and hope to keep doing so, on and off, until the great final curtain call is ordered from on high.

23

I become Rector of two universities

Early in 2000 I was surprised to be approached by the then-president of Edinburgh University Students Association, who now works for the BBC, and asked if I would be willing to stand for election as Rector of the then 618-year-old university.

The Lord Rector of the University of Edinburgh is elected every three years by the students and staff. The primary official role of the Rector is to chair the University Court and, when the Chancellor is absent, the General Council. The current Chancellor, since 1953 and for life, is Queen Elizabeth's husband, Prince Philip, the Duke of Edinburgh. More importantly, perhaps, the Rector is an ombudsman for the university community, working particularly closely with the various students' associations.

It is a great honour to be elected to the post. At least three British prime ministers, Winston Churchill, William Gladstone and Gordon Brown, have been Rectors of Edinburgh University, together with such luminaries as the historical and satirical essayist Thomas Carlyle, the discoverer of penicillin, Sir Alexander Fleming, and Lord Kitchener of Khartoum, the British field marshal who won fame securing the Sudan and South Africa for British rule.

I of course fancied adding my name to this list, but there were a few questions I needed to ask the students and myself. Having first ascertained that the university's People and Planet Group, a dynamic student activist organisation with 40 years' experience of campaigning to end world poverty, defend human rights and protect the environment, was likely to support me, I gave a tentative yes. Given how high-profile past Rectors had been, I thought that the competition would make it a very difficult contest to win. But then I decided it would be fun, and it would be a big boost to the Green Party if I won; and if I lost it probably would not do the party much harm. So I signed an acceptance form.

The weeks passed and in late March I travelled to Faslane, the naval base on the west coast of Scotland that is home to Britain's fleet of nuclear submarines armed with Trident missiles, each with a range of 7,000 miles and armed with three nuclear warheads, to take part in a routine Campaign for Nuclear Disarmament demonstration. It was bitterly cold and dark and wet at 5am, but by 11 it was beautifully sunny and I took an offer of a lift back to Edinburgh by Scottish National Party MSP Linda Fabiani. My mobile rang and it was the university's deputy secretary, Melvyn Cornish, who said: 'I thought you'd like to know that as there has been no other nomination for Rector as of midday today you are de facto the elected Rector of Edinburgh University. I look forward to seeing you at your installation. Congratulations.'

Since I had been on an anti-nuclear protest at a site where police sometimes take action against demonstrators, I could just possibly have been the first Edinburgh University Rector to be arrested. I am just ever so slightly disappointed that I was unable to claim this as another Harper 'first'!

I was also a bit disappointed at the easy win. I would have liked a contest. Rectorial elections when I was an undergraduate at Aberdeen University were great fun, with a hugely complicated system of voting culminating in a battle in the quad of 400-year-old Marischal College between rival teams armed with bags of flour and the lungs and other bits of offal from animals slaughtered in local abattoirs. I remember once being struck by a length of the oesophagus of a horse and a bit of its lung that wrapped themselves around my neck and brought me to the ground. Since the 1990s, when the culture of health and safety began taking hold in Britain, the animal parts have been barred from battle and only the bags of flour are now permitted.

In the 19th century the Rector of Aberdeen University used to be installed in the concert hall in Union Street in the centre of the city. The students processed along the street armed with peashooters which they fired at the local people and at each other. When the city and university banned the peashooters, students responded by taking mushy peas – soaked overnight in water and then simmered with a little sugar and salt until they form a thick green lumpy porridge – into the hall and staged a pitched battle with them that resulted in so much damage to the paintwork that the concert hall had to be redecorated. The students were permanently banned from the hall.

* * *

My installation as Rector at Edinburgh University was quite a thrill. After the ceremonial entry of the university staff, I gave the traditional Rectorial Address in which, naturally, I said Green had to be the colour of the 21st century for the health and survival of our planet.

'We only need to look back a little way to see that in recent history humankind has become the single greatest force of nature – and a malignant force at that,' I said.

The late Gerald Durrell[1] described the world as being as delicate and complicated as a spider's web. If you touch just one thread, you send shivers running through all the other threads.

We are not just touching the web. We are tearing holes in it. The latest research suggests that it would take ten million years for the earth to repair the damage we have done already.

By the time I was elected Edinburgh Rector Mum had passed away. But Pa was there and he was so chuffed that I caught sight of him in tears of joy as I was 'robed up' in the Rector's plush full-length red gown, with black sleeves and gold facing, together with a plum-coloured beret-like hat, by the University Principal, Sir Stewart Sutherland, a fellow undergraduate and contemporary of mine at Aberdeen University. Pa had already written to say how proud he was of me and how he was beginning to share my views on the environment and what we needed to do to make the world a better place. It is one of the best

---

[1] Gerald Durrell was a naturalist, zookeeper, conservationist, author and television presenter. Founder of the Durrell Wildlife Zoo on the Channel Island of Jersey, his many books include the brilliant *My Family and Other Animals*, *A Zoo in My Luggage* and *The Garden of the Gods*.

and most moving letters I received from my father who throughout his life kept in touch with me regularly with letters and postcards from wherever Navy life took him. Afterwards I was carried from the assembly hall in the Rector's very grand chair atop a wooden trestle on the shoulders of eight strong undergraduates.

I threw myself into the Rectorship role. The University was going through a staffing upheaval. Some of this was quite painful and I was involved in quite a few appeals by lecturers facing redundancy. By and large the University's human resources department managed things well, but however good the system is you cannot take away the pain from somebody who has served for 25 years and suddenly finds his or her job has been downgraded or is being offered an early pension well before thinking of retiring. Some complaints by students were completely intractable: there were people who refused to take no for an answer when told they had failed their degree.

One of my primary concerns was the welfare of students, a result directly of my previous work as a guidance teacher and my own Diploma in Guidance and Counselling from Edinburgh University. My investigations showed that the University counselling service and the students' own voluntary nightline and counselling operations were good. But I was concerned that perhaps too few students knew that the services existed. I suggested that every student be given a business-size card with the phone numbers of the student nightline, the Samaritans, the student counselling service, the student health service and various other useful numbers. The measure was adopted and has since been taken up in one form or another by many of Scotland's other universities.

Edinburgh had in 2000 gained an unfair reputation as the student suicide capital of Scotland, mainly as a result of some over-the-top reporting by newspapers. One member of staff and two students had committed suicide that year, which was three too many. They included 22-year-old Stephanie Bramsen, the daughter of Denmark's ambassador to China, who was in the final year of an English honours degree and who had played international rugby for Scotland's women's team. Stephanie's mother, Dr Michele Bo Bramsen, a university lecturer in France, said her daughter was depressed, in the aftermath of a failed love affair, when she plunged to her death from the university's ugly 10-storey Appleton Tower. Dr Bramsen said her daughter's death made her think it was not enough to offer counselling to students about feelings of isolation and alienation – services needed to reach out and offer nurturing rather than wait for them to make an approach.

Among reasons for my concern about sensational reporting was that studies had shown that over-publicisation of suicides can lead to copycat suicides. A spate of 25 suicides in a short period of time in 2007 by young people in the Bridgend area of South Wales raised concerns that networking sites on the internet had encouraged these intentional self-killings. All hanged themselves, except for one 15-year-old who lay down on the tracks before an oncoming train. One of those who hanged himself was 20-year-old Thomas Davies. He had been friends with David Dilling, 19, and Dale Crole, 18, who had been found dead weeks earlier. Thomas's mother, Melanie Davies, said: 'For the kids, I think they should talk to somebody, even if it's a stranger. They really need to speak to somebody, even if it's over the phone.' Darren Matthews, Bridgend director of The Samaritans, which offers emotional support for people in distress or at risk of suicide, said he was convinced the series of suicides was down to copycat behaviour resulting from publicity surrounding the deaths.

Psychologists familiar with the phenomenon say that what happened in Bridgend was a classic case of the Werther effect, named for the novel *The Sorrows of Young Werther* by Johann Wolfgang von Goethe, the German writer and polymath. The novel is about a young man who put a gun to his head to end the agony of unrequited love and because he could not find his place in the provincial bourgeois society of the day. The novel's publication, in 1774, prompted young men all over Europe to dress like Werther and take their own lives. The phenomenon is called the contagion effect as well as copycat suicide: one person does it, and that lowers the threshold, making it easier and more permissible for the next. It's like 10 people waiting at a pedestrian crossing for the light to go green, when one of them jaywalks. This gives the rest of them the go-ahead.

Tabloid reporters descended on Bridgend, and the story went national, then international, in less than a week. The sudden global attention precipitated – or permitted – four hangings over the next month.[2] The Bridgend suicides illustrated the fact that the suicide problem in Britain is less among students as among young people aged 15–25 generally not at university. Of the total 746 officially recorded suicides in Scotland in 2009, the anti-suicide agency Choose Life commented:

> Suicide rates generally increased with increasing deprivation, with rates in the most deprived 30 per cent areas of Scotland significantly higher than the Scottish average. Despite commendable initiatives, Government and care agencies have still not yet done enough to address this tragic situation arising mainly among youngsters who have either been in care, or in trouble with the police, or involved in drugs or out of work.[3]

Together with the university staff I expressed concern about the way newspapers reported the limited number of Edinburgh University suicides. I think Scotland's newspapers have since begun to show more respect for the feelings of families of young people who take their own lives.

Working as Rector with the Scottish Association for Mental Health, with the Edinburgh University Health Centre, the students' association and Parliament's own cross-party group on mental health, of which I was vice-president for a time, I managed to get a greater acceptance that student mental health deserved special attention. I contended that these were young people experiencing a serious transition point in their lives, many of them very far away from home and among them the reticent and shy who find it difficult to make friends and settle and are therefore vulnerable.

*   *   *

In 2005 I was elected for a three-year term as Lord Rector of my old university, Aberdeen. This time I won a contest against a local media

[2] 'The Mystery Suicides of Bridgend County', by Alex Shoumatoff in *Vanity Fair*, 27 February 2009.
[3] Choose Life is the Scottish Government's strategy and action plan to prevent suicide. Its website is: www.chooselife.net

figure and, as at Edinburgh, I again followed in the footsteps of Winston Churchill who was Aberdeen University's Rector throughout the First World War. In each year I addressed the new first-year freshers and made a point of mentioning mental health and provisions made by the university to assist anyone feeling down in any way. Because their new experience was meant to be the beginning of a new exciting chapter in their young lives, I did not make it too heavy, but I did refer to my own relatively modest experience of depression as an undergraduate.

The Aberdeen Rectorship was in many ways as enjoyable and eventful as that at Edinburgh, but was slightly more difficult because of the distance I had to travel from home in Edinburgh to attend Court and Council meetings and other functions. There was also the added problem that Aberdeen University at the time of my election had begun negotiations with the Privy Council, which oversees the governing instruments of the United Kingdom's universities, with a view to stripping the Rector of the automatic right to chair Court and other of the governing bodies through a change in the university statutes.

In the history of the world this was not the most important of issues, but I had promised the students that if elected I would chair Court. I therefore felt duty-bound to do so and made sure I continued to do so for the whole of my term of office. I do not know to this day how popular that was with the academics, and the Rector who succeeded me has stood down from chairing duties.

I keep my connections with Aberdeen and its university through lifelong friends such as Roddy Begg, a fellow undergraduate at the university in the late 1950s and early 1960s. Roddy became the university's Secretary, retiring just before I was elected Rector. I remember processing into King's College Chapel for my installation in the Rector's magnificent gold-fronted gown and gold-tasselled mortar board as Sir Duncan Rice, Aberdeen University's Principal, another undergraduate contemporary who I worked with when he was editor of *Gaudie*, the student newspaper, whispering to me: 'Robin, who would ever have *thunk* this?'

Given my particular undergraduate history and travails at Aberdeen, who indeed would ever have *thunk* it!?

24

Local Hero 2

In Scotland we need local heroes, lots of them – just like the spirited but impecunious Highlander on the west coast in the BAFTA award-winning movie *Local Hero* who refuses to sell his stretch of beach in the fictional fishing village of Ferness to a Texas oil magnate to make way for the construction of a refinery.

The American tycoon, played by Burt Lancaster, tries everything to entice the Highlander, Ben Knox, to sell, even offering enough money to buy any other beach in the world. But the old man refuses to budge. He is content with what he has.

In a happy ending, the magnate sees the error of his ways, abandons his refinery plan and agrees to finance an oceanographic institute to help conserve Scotland's marine and coastal wonders.

Well, sometimes truth proves stranger than fiction. As this book hit the shelves, a battle of epic proportions was intensifying in an attempt to persuade the New York property magnate Donald Trump to abandon his bulldozing of an exquisite stretch of Scottish coastline, home to all manner of wildlife, including otters, badgers, barn owls, buzzards, skylarks and rare plants and vegetation, to create a small town of nearly 1,500 flats and houses and an eight-storey hotel. These are to be set amid two golf courses, the first of which is being excavated and bulldozed and has already destroyed a unique sand dune system that enjoyed special protection under Scottish law.

The crusade against Trump, who bought the lairdship and Barony of the 1,400-acre Menie Estate, north of Aberdeen, stems from one of the great scandals of the four-year period of rule between 2007 and 2011 by Alex Salmond's Scottish National Party. For reasons that can only be surmised, Salmond and his ministers have overruled a local planning committee and given *carte blanche* to an American billion-aire to build houses for millionaires on precious and beautiful terri-tory, near the village of Balmedie, that should be conserved in its natural state for generations to come.

Step forward Michael Forbes, a 58-year-old salmon fisherman, farmer and granite quarry worker, a *real life* Local Hero who refuses to sell his 25-acre property, in the middle of the proposed Menie development, to Trump – despite the New Yorker's offers of buyouts worth hundreds of thousands of pounds. Trump, enraged by Forbes' determination to stay on his property, described the fisherman as a 'village idiot' for his refusal to budge. Piling insult on insult, he told reporters that Forbes and his 86-year-old mother live in 'disgusting conditions . . . a slum, a pigsty'.

Forbes, with his wry northeast Scotland humour and sense of the ridiculous, closely resembling Ben Knox as played by Fulton Mackay in the original *Local* Hero, riposted: 'If I'm the village idiot, he must be the New York clown . . . He's just a child. He's never grown up. I don't know why he's getting his nappy all in a knot. My land has been in my family for more than half a century. It belongs to me and never will belong to him.'

As Trump's battle against Forbes and other protesters evolved into an epic saga, I decided to give them my support. When Salmond's govern-ment overruled the Aberdeenshire Council decision and gave Trump the green light to forge ahead with his billion-dollar development, people responded to the executive diktat by forming the Tripping up Trump resistance group, with its own website[1], and bought an acre of Michael Forbes' land wanted by the American Republican and Tea Party sup-porter. Together with 62 campaigners, I was one of the founder deed holders in the property. If Trump wants our land, he will need to fight each one of us individually through the courts and will have huge legal and political difficulties for years and years. We invited others outraged by the conduct of the Trump entourage and the Salmond government to back The Bunker and as this book went to print thousands of supporters from around the world had signed up to The Bunker.

---

[1] www.trippinguptrump.com

I happily gave my support to the people who live at Menie in their fight against Orwellian corporate might. Trump, demonstrating an attitude that has angered swathes of Scots and others, said unilaterally that he had decided to rename the Menie sand hills The Great Dunes of Scotland, or, as he pronounced them, 'The Great Doons of Skatland'!

One of the recruits to what the resistance group has dubbed 'The Bunker' a tongue in cheek protest against Trump's planned eighth and ninth golf holes near Michael Forbes' property is David Puttnam, the producer of *Local Hero* and other outstanding movies, such as *Chariots of Fire*, for which he won an Oscar, *The Killing Fields*, *The Mission*, *Bugsy Malone*, *Midnight Express* and *Memphis Belle*. As he bought his portion of The Bunker acre, Puttnam told reporters: 'This saga is the real-life version of a film I made over 25 years ago. *Local Hero* had a happy ending when the American developer came to his senses and withdrew with dignity. It would be great if Trump would watch it.'

Others who gave support include Oscar-winning actress Tilda Swinton; Queen rock hero guitarist Brian May, who vowed 'to stop this nasty business in its tracks'; Dr Adam Watson, one of Scotland's most prominent environmental campaigners; and Gordon Roddick, co-founder of *The Body Shop International*, the second largest cosmetic franchise in the world, with 2,400 stores in 61 countries and a reputation for innovation, integrity and social responsibility.

Roddick commented: 'It is time to draw a line in the sand and not let the bully boys ride roughshod over decent people. Trump, like Murdoch [media mogul Rupert Murdoch, the world's largest publisher of newspapers], cares nothing for integrity or decency. I am happy to engage in action that will send them back to where they belong.'

Trump's business philosophy seems to be: If you have got enough clout, if you have got enough money, then you can buy anything or anyone. And if he cannot buy, he seems to resort to insults. Witness his attacks on Michael 'Local Hero' Forbes, of whom he said, in fractured grammar, in an interview with Scottish Television (STV), the country's largest independent TV broadcaster: 'I look at Mr Forbes and his disgusting conditions in which he lives, and that people have to look at that . . . It's almost like, in fact it is like, a slum-like condition. For people to have to look at this virtual slum, it's a disgrace. Mr Forbes is not a man that people in Scotland should be proud of. Mr Forbes lives in a pig-like atmosphere. It's disgusting.'[2]

Of Tilda Swinton, Trump said he had never heard of her but that she was obviously 'enjoying this publicity stunt at my expense'. Ms Swinton, who lives in the Scottish Highlands, compared Trump's attempt to push out Menie's small home and land owners to the Highland Clearances of the 18th and 19th centuries, when poor tenant farmers were brutally evicted and forced to emigrate by chieftains who turned cropland into vast pastures for sheep, providing meat and wool for the great burgeoning cities of the Industrial Revolution, and into moorland playgrounds supporting grouse and red deer, hunted and shot by the new industrial aristocracy.[3]

Commenting on fears that the Trump Organization and its supporters in the ruling Scottish National Party considered using compulsory purchase orders to crush resisters, Swinton, who can trace her ancestry back to Robert the Bruce, one of Scotland's greatest kings who waged guerrilla warfare against English invaders, said: 'Surely this kind of industrial bullying has been discredited enough. I trust Aberdeenshire Council to know its Highland history and to resist giving in to this attempt at a 21st-century clearance.' This inspired George Sorial, Trump's head of international development, to accuse The Bruce's heir of siding with 'extremists'.[4] Sorial also boasted that his and Trump's philosophy was: 'Progress happens. Real estate development happens.' My own riposte to Sorial is: 'Environmental destruction should not happen.'

I, along with many Scots, have been appalled by the way in which Trump has been making a mockery of Scotland's planning and environmental laws. When I bought my share in The Bunker I released a public statement saying: 'I decided to be a deed holder of this land as an investment in fairness and in the environment. Also to show that

---

[2] *STV News*, 24 November 2009.
[3] *Aberdeen Evening Express*, 16 October 2009.
[4] *The Scotsman*, 'Tilda on Trump: He's a Discredited Industrial Bully', 9 October 2009.

even minnows can challenge the rich and powerful. Occasionally the Law is on our side. We cannot allow ourselves to be bullied and trampled on by someone who is so rich that he has lost touch with the realities of life, lost touch with the way real people feel, and is so insulated from humanity that he cannot even begin to understand why we are all so upset.'

Another co-owner of The Bunker, Cameron McNeish, a prominent outdoor pursuits author and broadcaster, commented: 'I've been extremely concerned how a Site of Special Scientific Interest can be reduced to yet another piece of real estate when someone comes flashing enough money. Will Donald Trump ever learn that not everything has a cash value – that there are such things as aesthetics, love of a home, a love of wild land and, most important of all, a connection with an area of landscape that money can't buy? So far Aberdeenshire Council and senior Government politicians have acted in an abominable manner.'

＊　　＊　　＊

Having bought the Menie Estate, the Trump Organization assumed that it would be easy to buy up all the independent landowners within or on its boundaries. It was a mistaken belief. Michael Forbes is no lone Local Hero. Many others are standing up to fight and to make Trump think again. David Milne is a particularly strong and clear-thinking 'refusenik' who is determined not to be moved. Recalling when rumours began that Menie was about to be sold and flattened into golf courses, holiday apartments, residential houses and a hotel, 46-year-old Milne, a former North Sea oil rig worker, said: 'I got this phone call from a man calling himself Peter White who said, "I've been shooting on the Menie Estate and I've fallen in love with your house; would you consider selling it?" To which the answer was no. A couple of days later we found that everyone [other home owners] had had the same call. It turns out it was Trump's Menie project director Neil Hobday.

'I don't like liars. Can you really believe he thought we wouldn't talk to each other? I think he thought we are all as stupid as he is. He [later] appeared on the doorstep with some woman in tow who he said was his wife and I haven't seen since. This time he said, "You said you'd be interested in a really good offer." So I said, "No, I didn't, I said no," and shut the door in his face.'[5]

Milne's house, the last building at the end of a winding farm track, was a former coastguard station with very basic and rudimentary facilities. It was cold, damp and dilapidated. Milne bought the station, high on a bluff, from the government for £18,000 and converted it into an unusual four-bedroom, three-bathroom home with a conservatory, double garage, and a beautiful study in the station's former observation tower with windows on four sides. The house, now worth hundreds of thousands of pounds, has wonderful views across the marshy valley, or slack, behind the Menie dunes and over the dunes themselves to a wide vista of the North Sea where dolphins play.

Milne said he and his wife Moira immediately loved the house and its site, perhaps the most outstanding on the entire east coast of Scotland. 'It was peaceful and we were surrounded by nature, a place of remarkable beauty. At the time we got married we did ask ourselves if this was the right place or should we be looking for somewhere in town. But when we saw flats in Aberdeen or houses on estates in the outlying villages we realised that nothing compared to this. We didn't buy on a whim. We bought because we wanted to be here for ever . . . My intention at the end of the day is to leave here horizontally in a box. I can't make it any clearer than that.'

The Milnes' peace was disturbed when towards the end of 2010 Trump got permission to begin work on the first of his two golf courses. An army of heavy industrial equipment moved in to rip up wild land which had been largely undisturbed for thousands of years. Small lakes are being drained, land is being excavated to create car parks and orange plastic fences festoon the landscape, leaving terrible scars. Buzzards were still swooping across the area when Trump, with the Salmond government's permission, committed the ultimate act of environmental vandalism, bulldozing into oblivion a government-designated Site of Special Scientific Interest, or SSSI.

The law protects SSSIs from development, from other damage, and

[5] *Scotland on Sunday*, 12 September 2010.

also from neglect. Protection, unfortunately, is not absolute, and may be overridden by the government for such nationally important economic considerations as the building of a major road, a port or oil pipeline. In permitting Trump to destroy the Menie SSSI, the Salmond government abused the law, certainly in spirit, since the Trump golf course qualifies in no way whatsoever as 'nationally important'.

The SSSI the Milnes watched being destroyed below their home by Trump's bulldozers, excavators and trucks was a sheet of unique sand dunes that shift northwards each year by a few metres. Within them were tiny lakes surrounded by reeds that were home to innumerable birds. Local walker Erica Hollis regarded the area as an 'oasis', a 'mini-paradise'. She says she cannot bear to walk near the destroyed area any more. 'Why,' she asks, 'should any of us ever respect or value SSSI status ever again? A beautiful habitat evolved over hundreds, maybe thousands, of years was bulldozed away, obliterated under a mound of tangled tree roots and sand, in a single afternoon. I could have wept.'

David Bale, the area manager for Scottish National Heritage, the nation's environmental watchdog, said in August 2007: 'This site at Menie with its huge wild sand dunes is part of the largest dune system in Scotland. The Menie sand dunes are not like the majority of other UK sand dune areas – if they are not able to continue to shift and change, what makes them special will be lost. As the development of a golf course at this location would cause such significant damage to the Site of Special Scientific Interest, we (SNH) have maintained our objection to this part of the proposal. Building the championship golf course on the SSSI will inevitably damage it.'

Despite huge opposition, the support of the Scottish Government enabled Trump to destroy most of the protected dunes. Those parts he did not bulldoze he stabilised by planting marram grass and other plants, thus destroying their unique quality of being 'moving dunes'. Trump said with a typical mix of disdain, conceit and ignorance: 'We're saving the dunes! These dunes would have blown away if we hadn't done all this work.' And there were we environmentalists thinking the dunes had been just fine for tens of thousands of years without a tycoon's intervention!

Dr Jim Hansom, a Glasgow University lecturer in earth sciences and a former member of the SNH scientific advisory committee, said at an inquiry that the Menie SSSI site was the 'jewel in the crown' among British coastal sand dune systems. 'Within a Great Britain context, this long-lived dune movement has created a distinctive and unique set of landforms whose progressive northerly movement has left in their wake a series of ecological stepping stones back through time,' he said. Dr Hansom dismissed as 'rubbish' Trump's evidence to the same inquiry that the remaining dunes could have been 'blown away' unless they were stabilised.[6]

Milne's defiance earned him the fierce enmity of Neil Hobday, *alias* Peter White. When people were invited to a local hotel to see zoning diagrams of Trump's proposals, Milne vociferously criticised them, inciting Hobday to shout angrily in front of journalists: 'Pick your own platform. Pay for it somewhere else: invite the media and do it there. Just clear off. Clear off.'[7]

* * *

The Salmond government got involved in the Menie affair on Trump's behalf after Aberdeenshire Council's powerful infrastructure committee threw out the Trump Organization's planning application. The motion, binding on the whole council, was carried by eight votes to seven, with committee chairman Martin Ford, then a Liberal Democrat councillor, casting the deciding vote against Trump following a 7–7 tie among other councillors.

The infrastructure committee had been concerned that the Trump proposal should show respect for a 'fantastic natural environment', and was particularly worried about the threat to the mobile sand dune system. 'It was recognised this would be a serious loss to science, to north-east Scotland and to future generations,' said Councillor Ford. Committee members also queried the late inclusion in Trump's plans of a major residential housing development for open sale on rural land that had never been intended for this purpose. When Trump argued

[6] 'Golf plans threaten change of "biblical" scale"', *The Scotsman*, 19 June 2008.
[7] *The Scotsman*, 12 March 2010.

that the housing was necessary to fund other parts of the development, including the golf courses, 'there was concern about setting a dangerous precedent,' said Ford. When Trump threatened to build his golf course somewhere else in Europe unless he was permitted to bulldoze the SSSI, Ford said he realised 'we were having a pistol held to our heads, and that we could only permit the development if we sold our souls'.

All hell broke loose following the committee decision to refuse Trump's plans. Though it was widely reported as an outright rejection of any development, the committee had not in fact said absolutely: 'Go away.' It said: 'Make changes that are environmentally friendly.' Members of Aberdeenshire Council who favoured the Trump development but who were not on the committee were furious at what they saw as a total rejection of any development, and George Sorial, the Trump Organization's managing director for international development, said: 'I think it sends out a devastating message that if you want to do big business, don't do it in the northeast of Scotland.'

Now the fat was well and truly in the fire. Aberdeenshire, Scotland and the wider world divided bitterly for and against Trump. The committee decision to refuse the application was praised by conservationists and strongly condemned by business leaders and politicians beguiled by the Trump bling. Malcolm Bruce, the Liberal Democrat Westminster MP for the area, weighed in on the side of Trump, saying he hoped it would still prove possible to implement the American's plans for Menie. The Scottish Green Party's own Shiona Baird, based in northeast Scotland, countered that the planning decision meant that 'the people of Aberdeenshire have sent Donald Trump homewards to think again.'

Councillor Ford received hundreds of angry emails from Trump supporters, especially those in the business community. Ford, born in England, also received a handful of racist anti-English emails from people who disagreed with the infrastructure committee's decision. Both of the local papers, the daily Aberdeen *Press and Journal* and its sister paper, the *Evening Express*, heavily backed Trump. Liberal Democrat Councillor Debra Storr, who had voted against the Trump plans, was assaulted at her home by an angry pro-Trump woman who shouted obscenities. Storr was not injured and there was no prosecution.

The *Evening Express* launched an exceptionally vicious attack, in the style of rightwing American shock-jocks, on councillors who voted against the plans. Their photographs were run on the paper's front page under the huge headline 'YOU TRAITORS'. In an editorial, the newspaper described them as 'stupid', 'misfits', 'small-minded numpties', 'buffoons in woolly jumpers', 'no-hopers' and 'traitors to the northeast'. The *Evening Express* demanded that all the anti-Trump councillors resign and showed each of their heads as a turnip. It also gave their email addresses. Within hours Councillor Ford received hundreds more emails, some so threatening that the police advised him and his wife to stay at home and keep the doors of their house locked. It was a low and shameful example of Scottish journalism.[8]

Votes on the infrastructure committee had not been cast on party political lines. Its members made a regulatory decision that was procedurally impeccable, splitting for and against regardless of party. However, the atmosphere within the Liberal Democrat group on the full council became ever more poisonous, and the Liberal Democrat leader of Aberdeenshire Council, Anne Robertson, triggered an inevitable split when she backed Trump to the hilt and launched a campaign to overturn the decision rejecting Trump's application. In New York, Trump claimed there was 'rioting' in support of him in Aberdeenshire.

Councillor Robertson, who was not a member of the infrastructure committee, called a full meeting of Aberdeenshire Council to oust Martin Ford and to try to reverse the rejection of Trump's proposals. Trying to overturn the decision was as hopeless a task as spitting on a red-hot iron: the planning body had made its decision and the rules precluded any right to overrule it by the full council.

Meanwhile, Michael Forbes, speaking to reporters on his land, the Mill of Menie Farm and Fishing Station, amidst clucking chickens and squawking geese and directly adjacent to proposed fairways of Trump's golf course, was telling reporters he would never sell to

[8] *Evening Express*, 30 November 2007.

Trump, whatever price he was offered. 'I knew what kind of people they [the Trump team] were the first time I met them. People like Trump, they don't understand that there are some people who don't want lots of money. I've worked hard all my life to get this place and to keep it. What would I do with lots of money at my time of life?'

What if Trump offered him £10 million, the *Evening Express* taunted Forbes. 'He can shove it,' was the reply. 'He's pissed me off now. . . . He's a greedy man, that's all he is. We're just starting our fight now. They had better watch out.'[9]

*   *   *

The saga grew nastier and murkier.

The focus shifted heavily for a while from 'Local Hero' Forbes and his acres smack in the middle of Trump's development – with Forbes' barn walls emblazoned 'No Golf Course' and 'No More Trump Lies' in huge painted red letters – to Councillor Ford.

Journalists had a field day contrasting the bicycle-riding Ford, who has neither a car nor a driving license, with the American billionaire who regularly flies into Aberdeen aboard a jetliner with TRUMP outlined in giant gold letters along the aeroplane's fuselage to be greeted with a red carpet and a kilted bagpiper in full Highland regalia.

While few people wanted to read about the eye-watering intricacies of Scotland's planning laws and regulations, they were increasingly fascinated by the escalating war between the Menie residents and the egotistical billionaire with a controversial record on his American side of the Atlantic pond.

Trump's managing director for international development, George Sorial, began putting heavy pressure on the full Aberdeenshire Council to reconsider the planning decision – something, as Councillor Robertson discovered, it was not legally able to do. Under Scots law, only the national government could now reverse the decision, and only then under stringent conditions.

[9] *Washington Post*, 7 December 2007; London *Sunday Times*, 2 December 2007; *The Guardian*, 25 November 2007; *The Scotsman*, 22 November 2007; *New York Daily News*, 21 November 2007.

Having discovered that powers delegated to the committee could not be reversed, pro-Trump councillors plotted revenge. Some of Ford's own Liberal Democrat colleagues insisted he should resign his chairmanship of the infrastructure committee. He refused to cooperate in his own removal, arguing that it would set a dangerous precedent to get rid of the chairman of a planning committee simply for voting against a planning application when he had strictly followed all rules and guidelines. 'No-one was suggesting that I had acted in any way improperly or that I had erred procedurally when chairing the infrastructure services committee,' said Ford. 'Indeed, one cause of resentment was the *lack* of procedural errors because of the difficulty this presented to those who wanted to nullify the decision. As far as I was concerned, if I was to be removed this would be done in public, openly, where everyone could see how it was done and who did it.'

Sorial gave Aberdeenshire Council 30 days to reverse its planning authority's decision or the Trump Organization would take its giant golf course, hotel and housing development elsewhere. 'The clock is ticking,' Sorial warned councillors and officials. 'Some decision has to be made . . . If we have an option to build what we want in another place it may be a better business decision for us.'[10]

Bloggers galore hit newspaper opinion columns. 'Yes boss, OK bwana' was one typical response. 'This is tantamount to blackmail and shows up Trump to be an arrogant bully,' said another. 'What's next? A Trump-style casino on top of Ben Nevis?'; 'Trump wants to bully people into letting him do just what he wants; he does this in America all the time'; 'This is blackmail of the worst kind. How can we tell poor countries in Africa not to destroy habitat for endangered species if we can't even save a small patch of duneland?'; 'Why is Scotland pandering to the whim of a spoilt rich man?', said others.[11]

Pro-golf development councillors and Scottish government ministers, desperate for the Trump development, went into panic mode,

[10] *The Scotsman*, 'You've 30 days to do U-turn – Trump ultimatum to council', 4 December 2007.
[11] *The Scotsman*, 4 December 2007; 'Not the finest hour', Brian Taylor, *BBC Scotland*'s political editor, 13 December 2007.

taking actions that were ruthless and highly questionable on ethical grounds.

First Minister Salmond held emergency talks lasting nearly an hour with Trump's top representatives, George Sorial and Neil Hobday, at Aberdeen's Marcliffe Hotel. Many analysts argued that Salmond's meeting was strictly against rules barring Scottish First Ministers from becoming involved in planning inquiry decisions, either for or against a proposal. Salmond responded that he met Trump's men wearing his hat as an ordinary MSP, not as First Minister. It was a specious explanation, not least because towards the end of the meeting both Salmond and Sorial held a telephone conversation with the Scottish government's chief planner, Jim Mackinnon, in Edinburgh. It is stretching credulity to pantomime proportions to suggest that Trump's people did not realise that this 'humble' MSP was also the head of Scotland's government. Oh for one of Julian Assange's Wikileaks from this meeting!

The day following Salmond's Marcliffe Hotel meeting, his government 'called in', or overrode, Aberdeenshire Council's planning powers with regards to this application and later gave Trump the go-ahead. Never in the history of Scottish political devolution has there been such craven acceptance of a developer's proposal by our rulers.

Trump later said that someone high in Scotland's government had called him after his Menie dream was stymied by the Aberdeenshire planners to urge him to press onwards, assuring him: 'You'll win.' The tycoon said: 'I give the Executive [Salmond's government] a lot of credit. They called me and really wanted me to continue going forward. I said: Are you kidding? I just lost. I don't like to lose. They said no, you'll win. They didn't want me to leave.'[12]

Trump went on: 'I have a lot of respect for Alex Salmond. He loves Scotland above all else. I know he wanted the project to happen because it was good for Scotland.'

The Menie resisters felt contemptuous towards Salmond and his demonstration of support for the rich American at the expense of his

---

[12] *The Sun*, 18 October 2010; *Daily Mail*, 18 October 2010; *The Press and Journal*, 18 October 2010; *Scotland on Sunday*, 24 October 2010.

own fellow Scottish countrymen.[13] They also felt democratically unrepresented since the MSP for the area in which their homes were situated was Salmond himself. Labour MSP Duncan McNeil commented in a parliamentary debate: 'Cynics might say, "Trump said jump. The First Minister [Salmond] said, How High?"'[14]

Events moved fast following this bending of the rules.

Back in Aberdeenshire, pro-Trump members of the council moved to sack Martin Ford from his committee chairmanship and membership of other planning bodies. It was a highly controversial act, won on a minority vote. Twenty-six councillors voted for the removal of Ford and of the others 10 voted against and 29 abstained. While some councillors were strongly pro-Trump, in the noxious atmosphere that now blanketed Aberdeenshire Council's huge headquarters others went along with the victimisation or abstained because they feared the consequences of expressing sympathy with Ford.

The consequences for Ford were serious. A full-time paid councillor, he lost top-up income for his work as a committee chairman. He now decided to withdraw from his party and sit as an independent because so many of his fellow Liberal Democrats had either voted against him or declined to stand up to be counted. 'There comes a time when the sensible and dignified thing to do is to walk away,' he said at the time. 'I have been to one too many poisonous meetings. Frankly, life's too short.

'I was the subject of the most unpleasant witch-hunt. I was removed from a whole series of positions from the council after I was given assurances that I would not be. It was like being declared a "non-person" in the old Soviet Union. However you look at it, this is really a monstrous way to be treated.'

Before the vote was taken to remove Ford, the *Evening Express* reported under the headline 'We want "Trump traitor" sacked' that Aberdeen's top business leaders and company bosses had written to the chief executive of Aberdeenshire Council, Alan Campbell, calling for Ford to be ditched from his committee chairmanship, effectively

[13] *Scotland on Sunday*, ' "Government told me I'd win" Donald Trump,' 17 October 2010.
[14] *The Scotsman*, 'Trump said jump, Salmond said how high?', 25 April 2008.

asserting a right of veto over who could chair planning committees.[15] In a speech to the full council urging his colleagues not to remove him, Ford commented: 'The behaviour of the *Evening Express* has been widely described as disgraceful. Which of us is next? And how will we find people prepared to take tough decisions in the future if this is what they can expect?'

The Trump Organization's lack of understanding for local concerns about the environment was demonstrated when George Sorial said Ford and environmental campaigners had merely 'chosen to protect a pile of sand'.

* * *

Alex Salmond now felt free to speak openly about the Trump proposals. The First Minister said Trump would create 6,000 jobs, and added: 'The economic and social benefits for the northeast of Scotland substantially outweigh any environment impact. In tough economic times, substantial investment of this kind is at a premium.' Martin Ford accused Salmond of backing a 'vanity project', and went on: 'This is a very, very bad precedent indeed and sends out a bad message about the protection in Scotland of our natural heritage sites.' He added: 'For many years the [Aberdeenshire] council was worthy but dull – now it is neither. The democratic ethos has gone and with it equality of rights.'

* * *

Michael Forbes also reacted to the Scottish Government's decision to allow Trump's earth-moving equipment to move in on Menie and to a fresh offer from Trump of £450,000 for his property. 'I won't be moving,' Forbes warned. 'He's made a fool of the government, he's made a fool of the council, but he won't make a fool of me.' He said he was getting fan mail from across the world: 'They keep telling me to keep up the good fight. They just can't stand Trump: everything he touches turns to rubbish.' Blasting Aberdeenshire Council as 'Trump's puppets in action,' Scotland's latest Local Hero went on: 'It's a

---

[15] Aberdeen *Evening Express*, 6 December 2007.

vengeance thing now. It's become personal to Trump I think. He wants everybody who went against him all out, because he's a child.'[16]

In an amazing outburst, Trump hit back: 'Over the years, my representatives and I have often seen Mr Forbes and he has always been dirty, sloppy and unkempt in his personal appearance and demeanour.' This was so offensive that it should have resulted in the SNP government terminating Trump's enterprise with immediate effect. It was little wonder that Forbes was sometimes 'unkempt'. Unlike Trump, with his coiffed hair, manicured nails and designer clothes, Forbes earns his living with his hands in a quarry, casting nets at sea and caring for farm animals on his land. Trump compounded the insult by continuing: 'We will not be distracted by the rants of the local village idiot and intend to vigorously defend any challenge to our project. He (Forbes) is a loser who is seriously damaging the image of both Aberdeenshire and his great country.'

Forbes' neighbour David Milne said of the attack on his neighbour: 'It will maybe make some people who seem to think Trump is God's gift to this region look a little closer and understand why people across the world don't want him in the area.' And Martin Ford sighed that the American property tycoon's comments were 'the standard reaction from Mr Trump to anyone who stands up to him.'[17]

Still Trump piled verbal abuse upon Michael Forbes, saying: 'It's a very sad situation that his property is so badly maintained. It is a pigsty . . . The Scottish people are very clean people and yet this guy runs the property like a slum. He lives in squalor. He should clean up his property for himself and Aberdeen.'[18]

* * *

Work began on the first of Trump's two golf courses on Thursday 1 July 2010. As heavy machinery moved in notices went up saying: 'Keep Out. Unauthorised entry to this site is strictly forbidden.' Trump's security guards turned away any walkers who tried to

---

[16] *The Guardian*, 29 December 2008/1 September 2009; *The Scotsman*, 2 October 2009.
[17] *The Scotsman*, 25 November 2009.
[18] *The Herald*, 27 May 2010.

exercise their right to cross the 'Great Doons of Skatland', as established in 'right to roam' clauses in Scotland's 2003 Land Reform Act. Access to construction sites can be denied on grounds of safety, but the Trump Organization imposed a blanket prohibition beyond areas where work had begun.

The Trump labour force began erecting wooden chestnut paling fences to demarcate their boss's land from that of the small home owners holding out against the billionaire. They fenced for Trump a portion of Michael Forbes' land where he mended and dried his salmon nets. 'They've just come along, pushed everything off and put up a fence and said "to Hell with you,"' said Forbes, waving papers he carried showed the boundaries of his property. 'I have had that land since 1982 and my uncle had it since 1957. It's just not right.' Forbes then removed 25 red flags worth £10 each that Trump's men had planted to demarcate boundaries which Forbes asserted illegally 'stole' part of his land. The Aberdeenshire police charged him with theft of Trump's flags, and although he was given only a formal warning it meant he has a criminal record. 'I couldn't believe it when I was charged,' said the Local Hero. 'The flags were on my land, so I took them down to prove a point. As soon as the police turned up I handed them over. I am certainly not a thief. This is just another example of the Trump Organization trying to intimidate me.'[19]

Trump's workers also tightly surrounded David Milne's coastguard station house with wooden fencing and then, in what Milne and his supporters saw as a clear act of intimidation, dumped a small mountain of top soil tight up against the building and blocking Milne's open view to the north. Trump claims he has planning permission to build the soil mountain next to the home of Milne, who is appealing.

Angry readers' comments poured in to Scotland's newspapers and one of Scotland's finest journalists observed: 'Trumpland philosophy is simple. "When somebody hurts you," he once wrote, "go after them as viciously and violently as you can." '[20]

Just as it seemed the Trump saga could not become more outrageous,

[19] *The Scotsman*, 20 July 2010.
[20] *Scotland on Sunday*, 'The Catherine Deveney Interview,' 24 October 2010.

Aberdeen's Robert Gordon University, with a 260-year history and some 13,000 students, announced that the American would be given an honorary doctorate in recognition of his 'business acumen, entrepreneurial vision and the long-term future his company is planning in the northeast of Scotland.' The university's chief executive and principal, Professor John Harper, said: 'It is only fitting to award Mr Trump with an honorary degree. He is recognised as one of the world's top businessmen, and our students, the entrepreneurs of tomorrow, can learn much from his business acumen, drive and focus.'

Trump, with his egotistical behaviour in Scotland and a business record widely criticised in the United States, was an appalling example for Professor Harper to hold up to young people, and quickly the protests rolled in, including one from Dr David Kennedy, the university's principal for 10 years until 1997. Dr Kennedy returned the honorary degree he received in 1999, saying the decision to honour Trump was 'an insult to decent people everywhere'.

Handing back his degree in person to Professor Harper, Dr Kennedy told his successor: 'I was shocked and appalled at the decision to honour Donald Trump . . . I would not want to hold the award after Mr Trump has received his. He is simply not a suitable person to be given an honorary degree and he should not be held up as an example of how to conduct business.

'Mr Trump's behaviour in northeast Scotland has been deplorable from the first, particularly in how he has treated his neighbours. The university needs to realise how strongly people feel about this issue. I can think of no better way to express my anger at the decision to honour Mr Trump than to return my own honorary doctorate to the university.'[21]

Thousands of people signed a petition objecting to Trump's award, but on the day he received the degree, Sir Ian Wood, the powerful chairman of the Aberdeen-based Wood Group, one of the UK's largest engineering businesses, and chancellor of Robert Gordon University, told the American his degree was in recognition of 'your visionary world-class golf investment which, in spite of a vocal minority, is

---

[21] *Scottish Television*, 27 September 2010; *BBC Scotland*, 28 September 2010.

widely welcomed by the people of northeast Scotland.' This crass stuff
out of the mouth of Sir Ian came from a man once quoted as saying:
'I used to believe in a democratic system but really if you look at the
results yielded by democracy you realise most people don't know what
they are talking about. A select few should make informed decisions
for the masses.'[22] At least, this gave a clue about the kind of people
hidden in the corridors of power who were backing Trump.

* * *

In the summer of 2009 it became public that Trump was asking
Aberdeenshire Council to use its powers of compulsory purchase to
secure for the Trump Organization the land belonging to Michael
Forbes and others at Menie. Aberdeenshire Council now declined to
pass a proposed resolution that it surrender its right to use far-
reaching compulsory purchase orders. The council's refusal to abandon these powers set alarm bells clanging and anti-Trump resistance
rose to a new level of intensity.

A compulsory purchase order (CPO) is a directive in Scottish law
that gives a public body the power to take land or buildings against
owners' wishes for purposes including demolition and redevelopment.
Its use is generally reserved to allow the building of public infrastructure but can be used to allow 'the orderly planning of an area'. Its
human victims do have the right of appeal against eviction, but I have
never before heard of an instance where a CPO has been used to
facilitate the development of a leisure resort.

Realising that Aberdeenshire Council and Trump were reserving the
right to use CPOs against them, residents struck back on two fronts.

Families fearing the tycoon's plans to 'steal' their land in a modern-
day version of the Highland Clearances petitioned the Scottish government to tighten the law and remove the threat of CPOs being used
for private and predatory commercial developments. David Milne,
speaking for the residents, said: 'Now they're coming in simply with
heavy-handed bullyboy tactics – "we're the big boys here, we've got
the resources, we've got the back-up from Alex Salmond and powerful

[22] *Wikipedia*, the free encyclopaedia, 18 January 2011; *The Guardian*, 9 October
2010.

people behind the Aberdeenshire Council, we're going to take your land from you whether you like it or not."

'The Trump saga in Aberdeenshire has revealed many things – that neither local government nor Scottish ministers can be relied upon to stand up either for Scottish residents or our unique natural environment, that Mr Trump's ego will not compromise with anyone, and that the Scottish planning system is skewed in favour of developers no matter how ill-conceived their project may be.

'Why should a private developer be allowed to apply to demolish homes he does not own for his own profit?'[23]

Michael Forbes again told Trump 'to take his money and shove it up his arse'. But his 86-year-old mother, Molly Forbes, who lives in a chalet named 'Paradise' on Michael's acres, decided to take the Trump proposals to Scotland's highest court to have them thrown out, arguing that legal planning procedures had not been properly followed by Scotland's government.

Molly, as a pensioner and widow, was banking on receiving legal aid – which allows people who would not otherwise be able to afford it to get financial help for their legal problems – in her fight against the billionaire. Surprisingly, the Legal Aid Board refused Molly's request. Judge Alexander Wylie, whose judicial title is Lord Kinclaven, ruled heartlessly in Edinburgh's Court of Session that she had to pay Trump's and Aberdeenshire's expenses which were variously estimated at anywhere between £20,000 and £75,000.

Molly, who did not have that kind of money, said she would have to pay Trump at a penny a week. 'If he's a billionaire, what does he need money for from little people like me? He's unbelievable,' she said. 'It was very, very peaceful before Trump came. I wish he'd go. I wish he'd up and away.

'Going after me, a little person, a pensioner, it must make him look terrible. This is my home and I love it. He'll have to carry me out.'

Molly, with the support of her lawyers and from me, the Green Party and many other supporters, was not finished with Trump. Her

[23] *Guide and Gazette*, 8 January 2011; *BBC Scotland*, 7 January 2011; Aberdeen *Press and Journal*, 8 January 2011.

lawyers returned to the Court of Session to contest Lord Kinclaven's verdict waving the Aarhus Convention, an admirable European Union law overriding British law – somehow overlooked by Lord Kinclaven – that states there should be no prohibitively expensive barrier to justice in environmental matters. The convention entered into force in 2001 and goes to the heart of the relationship between people and governments, enforcing government accountability, transparency and responsiveness. It was a massive victory against the huge powers of Scotland's government and Establishment. The Legal Aid Board was forced to review its earlier decision and Molly Forbes vowed to fight Trump 'to the bitter end'.

I was in the Court of Session on 11 January 2011 when Molly won the right to have the Board members think again. I told reporters it was an outrage that she had been denied aid in the first place, and went on: 'I am pleased to offer my support to Molly and the many others who just wish to live without the cloud of eviction hanging over them, by buying, along with others, an acre of land belonging to Molly's son Michael Forbes.

'This should hopefully hamper any further eviction on Mr Trump's behalf, whose bullying tactics have been utterly disgraceful.'[24]

* * *

The Trump/Menie Estate scandal rumbles on and was likely to have serious consequences for the Scottish National Party and the Liberal Democrats when voters went to the polls to elect Scotland's fourth modern Parliament in May 2011. Opinion polls showed both these parties trailing well behind the opposition Labour Party.[25]

Following the controversy over the infrastructure committee vote, Martin Ford and fellow former Liberal Democrat councillor Debra Storr joined the Green Party. Widespread disillusion with the stand taken on Menie by the SNP and some Liberal Democrats, together with misgivings about the Liberal Democrats' coalition with the Conservative Party

---

[24] *The Herald*, 12 January 2011; *ClickGreen* website, 11 January 2011; *The Herald*, 3 November 2010.

[25] *Bloomberg*, 17 January 2011; *Press Association*, 18 January 2011; *The Herald*, 18 January 2011.

at Westminster, offered the Green Party a huge opportunity to gain seats in Aberdeenshire. Martin Ford, who refused to be blinded by the bling of the Trump corporate army, stood as our top candidate in the region: it seemed certain to be the most exciting of all the election battles. I was booked to make campaign appearances on behalf of Martin.

As this book went to print, Trump blinked. He said he was no longer seeking compulsory purchase orders to acquire the homes of local hero Michael Forbes and others. It was a real victory for those who wish to protect the Menie dunes and their unspoilt beauty. Trump, in withdrawing the threat, could not resist another unpleasant jibe, accusing Michael Forbes and others of having gained 'free publicity on the back of the Trump name' and having 'damaged Scotland's international business reputation'.

But new battles lie ahead. If Alex Salmond were to fall from power, as seemed likely at the time of writing, Donald Trump had better beware. Many people think along the lines of David Milne, who feels particularly badly let down by Salmond, his own MSP. 'Salmond is tainted by his behaviour and his adoration of Donald Trump,' said Milne. 'His behaviour in running after Trump raises questions and shows he is biased. He is also not willing to support his own constituents. I will not be voting for him in any future election.'[26] A new Scottish government and new Parliament, with more Green Party representatives, will not be so abjectly supportive of the bully from New York.

The most frustrating aspect of this entire affair is that the actions of the Aberdeenshire Council, Scotland's government and the Trump Organization have remained within the letter of the law, but not its spirit. It is the awful truth that our planning system does not protect local interest, offers little protection in the final analysis to the environment, and allows anyone with deep enough pockets to ride a coach and horses through it.

At the heart of this saga is the integrity of citizens' rights, the security of their homes, the Scottish people's right to roam and the true meaning of 'public interest'. It is also about the readiness and resolve of those who govern us to defend those rights against the hard-nosed encroachment of private power and wealth.

---

[26] *The Times*, 18 October 2009.

Epilogue

It has been said that the best way to predict the future is to invent it. The philosophy underpinning all Green thinking is the imperative to look far beyond the normal political horizons and into the distant future. Most politicians would freely admit that they limit themselves to tackling immediate problems using tools that are closest to hand. Green thinkers throughout the world, by contrast, have set themselves targets well beyond the next five years – targets that, if met, will stabilise our economies, produce fair trade worldwide, and hopefully, by so doing, remove many of the tensions that could lead to another half century of armed conflicts across the globe.

We all look for and enjoy those small things that give extra meaning to our lives – whether coincidental or purely accidental. Accidents have been the genesis of many of our most significant inventions, from vulcanised rubber to penicillin, but these accidents were only noticed because of the long-term dedication of their observers to the course they were following. It is not what happens to us that is important, it is how we react to it. And how we react is determined by our mindset, our commitment and our willingness to absorb new ideas.

What immediately appealed to me about Green thinking was that it asked a different set of questions – and if you do not ask the right questions you will never get the right answers. Faced with a new industrial process or a construction project or the development of a new technology, our first questions are not: 'Will this increase GDP?' 'Will it provide people with an easier life?' or 'Will it make something cheaper?' The immediate Green questions are: 'Will it damage the environment?' 'Will it improve our environment?' 'Will we be more relaxed or happy?'

It is all summed up in the holistic question: 'Is it environmentally sustainable and human scale?' It means working out what the 'win-wins' are for any policy. Here are a few examples of how I believe Green policies can really work.

Localism

This buzzword has been around in Green politics for maybe 20 years and is now creeping into the vocabulary of other political parties and even national institutions. Given some form of power, strengthening of local communities would be high on the list of Green Party policies. How would they look?

An administration inspired by Green policies would devolve much more responsibility to community councils, give them proper budgets within which they could decide their own expenditure, and we would bequeath to them a sound electoral process. Among decisions devolved would be aspects of management of public space, allotments and gardens, street furniture, placing of bus stops and waste bins, even responsibility for the 'look' of their communities – shop façades and so forth. Community recycling schemes in many parts of Scotland have been hugely successful and there is no reason why community councils and schools should not be encouraged to play a big part in boosting recycling. The city of Edinburgh pays £7 million a year in landfill tax. Think what could be achieved if this money were devolved to community councils or schools instead as part of a Zero Waste campaign.

Community energy scheme ideas are high on the Green agenda. We need to investigate how much carbon could be saved by local combined heat and power schemes, small or large scale, that could provide electricity and heat to communities at combined prices well below current market prices.

Local food policies would involve public and education services collaborating to buy food from local sources wherever possible, the promotion of farmers' markets, the expansion of allotments and encouraging those with gardens to devote ever more space to growing their own vegetables.

Local justice would mean that wherever possible sentences for minor crimes would be carried out through community service orders to the benefit of local communities and at a huge saving to the public purse. Restorative justice policies would also mean that people who had committed crimes against the person and the community would meet with the victims and they would listen to each others' stories. Both these strategies, when applied, have proved to be extremely effective in cutting re-offending rates and giving genuine comfort and closure to victims, while at the same time saving countless tens of thousands of pounds a year in the costs of the alternative prison sentencing strategies.

The setting up of Home Zones – areas where maximum speeds are at 20 mph (30 kilometres per hour) or less – would make life hugely easier for older people and children and the introduction of Land Value Taxation (described later) would encourage the development of small, local shopping streets. It is simply wrong that in Scotland the 40 per cent of those who do not own cars have so little easy access to places where they can buy life's daily necessities.

In schools, children should be consulted on any local decisions that affect them and under Green policies they would be enabled to become closely involved in local activities such as care of parks, working in allotments and volunteering.

We all too often focus on big – though undoubtedly important – issues but ignore our immediate environment. I remember a very enjoyable visit to a little school outside Edinburgh where I had been invited to speak and answer questions about the environment and to compliment them on a hugely detailed and thorough research project they had done on the Amazon River. They had clearly understood the major environmental challenges and were hugely enthused by the beauty and complexity of the life forms that they had discovered from insects through to snakes and small mammals. Though I was hugely impressed, I did ask the teacher if she had ever taken the class out of the school and into the woodland that lay about half a mile, or 10 minutes' walk, away, on the brow of the hill above the school. She said no: unfortunately they had to fill in so many forms for the risk assessment to get clearance that it did not seem worth it. It reminded

191

me of a story from another school where a keen young teacher had wanted to take her class out to do some bark rubbings in the local park. Her risk assessment form was returned with the injunction that as the children 'might catch something' off the bark, they would all have to be issued with industrial rubber gloves before they could rub the bark! This kind of lunacy and ultra-caution is restricting and stunting the outdoor experiences that are the right of every child. Localism in education means that we should allow children to explore and learn from the huge resources of their local environment wherever possible, in preference to picking up a book in the classroom on the same subject.

Localism is one kind of future I and Green thinkers intend to invent.

Our soil

Soil quality is fundamental to Green thinking on a range of policies, including agriculture, forestry, wildlife, water and housing. We cannot continue discussing and planning for these in separate boxes.

With the exception of only a few genuine wilderness spaces left, most of Scotland's land is totally subject to human control. If soil conservation becomes one of the basic principles of our land policy, we cannot go too far wrong. To hold the soil that we have in place we need more trees, especially in Highland river catchments and riverine environments where trees can stabilise river banks, expand wildlife habitats and provide shelter belts for agriculture and housing. One consequence would be less flooding and, in particular, less flash flooding, if we also paid farmers decent rate, to reinstate water meadows rather than paying town councils to erect concrete embankments that only shift the problem to other parts of the river.

A scientific soil conservation policy would recognise that healthy soils are rich in biodiversity, containing many tens of thousands of useful bacteria, spiders, worms and innumerable minute organisms that help to keep the soil alive and healthy. This would be an important step in the direction of reducing the use of chemicals: in itself it would result in a recovery of the natural wild plant and flower cover. Our honey and bumble bee populations are currently suffering serious losses. Given that between 20 and 30 per cent of our farmed crops rely on bees to pollinate them, we are facing a possible ecological, agricultural and economic disaster. A proper scientific soil conservation policy would go far towards addressing this problem.

Organic farming is not just about safeguarding our own land, it is also about stabilising and guaranteeing the future of food production throughout the world. I get infuriated by suggestions that organic farming is somehow going back to a pre-scientific era in which nature will simply take over. On the contrary, organic farming is about really understanding how soil works in a deeply scientific way and then using available natural processes to increase productivity, soil stability and health. An organic farmer needs to know a lot more than how to read the instructions on a sack of nitrate fertilisers.

Many people accuse Green thinkers of being anti-scientific. This is far from the truth – many scientific and technological advances contribute hugely to our comfort and well-being on this planet and can improve our environment. Green thinkers resist genetic modification of crops (GM), to take one scientific advance, for quite another reason: the history of GM development suggests that it has been designed solely for the financial benefit of certain big companies – for example, Monsanto, the United States-based multinational agricultural biotechnology company which provides the technology in 90 per cent of the world's genetically engineered seeds. Monsanto's development and marketing of genetically engineered seed and bovine growth hormone, as well as its aggressive litigation, political lobbying practices, seed commercialisation strategies and 'strong-arming' of the seed industry, have made the company controversial around the world and a target of protests by coerced poor Third World farmers and environmental activists.

It is clear from the activities of Monsanto and similar companies in the many corners of the globe where they have established a hold that they have little thought for anything other than their own profits. How else could they justify patenting their crops, not allowing farmers to store grain from these crops for use as future seed as they have done traditionally and tying all their products to their own brands of pesticides, fungicides and herbicides? The terms of use of these seeds mean farmers are forced to buy fresh seed each season from the company. Worse still, these packages need to be constantly updated as nature learns to resist the initial genetic concoctions – and so the cash will keep on rolling into the balance sheets. Eating GM foods is unlikely to affect our health in any way. It is the economics, the threat to the poor and the threats to the environment that are inherent in the use of many of the advanced GM technologies that deeply concern me.

The best future for both ourselves and the developing world will come from the spread of knowledge of advanced low-input and organic farming techniques, reinforced by traditional plant breeding and developments in storage to reduce the huge wastage of food after it comes out of the ground.

Soil conservation is one kind of future I would like to invent.

Energy and waste

By 2050, we need to have cut our use of fossil-fuel energy by 80 per cent. For the last 20 years Greens have engaged heavily in the fuel generation debate – what kinds of renewable energy systems we should be concentrating on, whether nuclear power can be counted as a renewable, how quickly we can get rid of coal-fired power stations. However, there are several important considerations from which we have been diverted in the course of battle.

No-one has questioned the wisdom of using up our gas reserves to make electricity. Without combined heat and power equipment, burning gas to produce electricity is one of the most horrendously wasteful things that we do at present, especially in winter. The efficiency losses mean that we are wasting at least 30 per cent of the energy that we could be getting from the gas. We would be far better burning it directly at home for heating and cooking.

The missing piece in the jigsaw is energy *conservation*. Greens are giving this maximum attention, while other politicians are blind to the huge benefits conservation offers. It is beyond belief that, with everything we know, we are filling our houses with electrical equipment, much of which is horrendously inefficient. The remedy for this is within the powers of the European Union. If we want to invent a future where you cannot buy inefficient electrical or gas appliances, all that is necessary is an EU directive (law) to restrict their manufacture and sale. Of all elections, those to the European Parliament stir the least amount of interest in the media and the population in general. This is a real shame because the European Parliament has real powers over the environment and we should be lobbying our Members of the European Parliament to do their utmost to improve European legislation.

Being a War child, another area of waste that maddens me is the amount of food we simply chuck in the bin. Over-reliance on refrigeration and weekly mass buys of food in Britain result in a 30 per cent wastage of all the food that we buy, most of it before it even hits our plates. We simply cannot afford to carry on squandering the world's resources in this way – we have to learn to buy only what we need and buy locally produced food wherever possible.

I also despair at supermarket two-for-one deals and vegetables packaged on plastic trays when I only want to buy a lesser loose quantity, while produce that *is* loose rarely identifies what variety it is or where it is from. It is so refreshing in Italy and France to find supermarkets that incorporate stalls where local farmers sell their fresh products more or less straight out of the ground. Why not here?

I have demonstrated outside the biggest supermarket chain in Britain against over-packaging and although supermarkets have responded in a limited way, I am sure that the most significant proportion of domestic waste going to landfill remains supermarket packaging. We pay twice for this ridiculous profligacy – once to the supermarkets and again to government in landfill taxes. We should all remove superfluous food packaging before leaving the supermarket and say, 'This is a problem you have created, you deal with it.'

A co-ordinated policy of waste reduction, energy conservation and renewable energy generation is one kind of future I would like to invent.

Green taxation policies

One Green idea that other politicians pick up, examine, then discard – probably on the basis that it's too disarmingly simple to work – is that of a basic income for citizens. We already have benefits that are as of right and automatic – child benefits, winter fuel allowance and, of course, the state pension. Many other benefits depend either on your state of health or whether or not you are in work. It is widely recognised that the system is hugely bureaucratic, cumbersome and has created what is now called the poverty gap. It is a cruel anomaly that sometimes parents with children who want to work will, for the sake of their children, stay out of work because they receive more benefit money and so are able to provide their children with greater comfort. Basic income is such a simple idea. All children would get an allowance (as they do already). All disabled people would get an allowance (as they do already). The difference is that everybody else would also get an allowance – as of right. The system would mean higher taxation, which no-one likes. However, all we need to do is look northwards to Norway and Sweden to learn that despite much higher tax rates, people are happier and certainly healthier than we are in Britain. Research seems to show that countries that allow huge pay differentials become unhappy societies. It is difficult to speculate on the reasons, but almost certainly higher levels of envy, resentment, tension and feelings of not being treated equally or fairly are part of it. So far, Norway and Sweden have managed to avoid this pitfall – very few people in those countries earn more than seven times the average wage.

Green thinkers also support the concept of Land Value Taxation (LVT), which places a community value on land that can be varied depending on the outcomes the communities are looking for. The banding would be according to use and could be varied in quite a sophisticated way. In the United States, there is no universal application of LVT, but quite a few cities have taken up the option so that, where vacant land is concerned, the community may zone it for specific uses and then apply the tax to that land whether it is in use or not. If someone owns some land that is scheduled for housing, or industrial development, or a shopping mall, they will pretty quickly start investing in the land rather than keeping it in a land bank. If the community wishes to encourage the development of small shops, they can lower LVT on land designated for such use, in order to produce the desired result. There are many other advantages to LVT – not the least of which is that it will tend to keep land prices under control and therefore keep house prices down.

Rethinking the way in which we raise taxes is one kind of future I would like to invent.

Our society

Many people think of Greens as simply being 'environmentalists' without understanding that, for us, 'getting it right' with the environment means looking at *everything* that surrounds us and seeing how we can improve it. This very much includes our communities and our society as a whole. All Green policies are thought through within the context of the questions 'Is it environmentally sustainable and human scale?' and 'Is it holistic?' We think of children, of parents, of older people and of the worlds of work and leisure in these contexts just as much as we consider the wider welfare of our planet.

We have to recognise that Scotland and Britain as a whole, more than 50 years after the end of World War Two, have still got huge problems of poverty. Sociologists have identified 50 districts in Scotland's towns and cities of multiple deprivation, poor housing, ill health, poor education, high levels of drug addiction, alcoholism, obesity, low life expectancy and high levels of social stress.

Politicians representing such deprived areas resent the implication that there is any connection between poverty and other social ills besetting these communities. On an individual basis, of course, it is quite true that being poor does not make one criminal, but the evidence staring us in the face is that if we create poverty ghettos – which is what we have done in many of our housing estates and high-rise blocks – the concentration of generational hopelessness and dysfunctionality has a corrosive and cumulative effect, and you cannot just throw money at it. Where we have started, slowly, to rebuild and refurbish the results have often been stunningly effective. Fairfield in Perth, to name just one estate, was not only run down but also being abandoned as fast as people could get out of it. An imaginative refurbishment of the Fairfield housing and some good landscape architecture has got people queuing to move back in.

You only have to contrast the worst of our housing estates with some of the quite ordinary middle-class areas of our cities to see how deep the divisions within our society have become. It resembles apartheid. This is a division that has actually been planned and constructed without any thought for the creation of communities or sense of place that are a necessary basis for people to live happily together.

My favourite charity is Children First and I have often said that you can judge society by what it does for its children and for its older people. One of the best things that has happened within government is the move towards a commitment to a 'getting it right for every child' strategy. There absolutely has to be all-party commitment to this with genuine long-term planning across all departments. If we accept that we need better conditions for children to live in, more people trained to work with and for families – in particular young mothers – and if we accept that every single public department has a part to play, we will soon realise that this is going to be a very long haul. But there is no excuse for a slow start.

Adopting an overall Green mindset of long-term planning is essential. In the case of children, I believe that simply by training and employing more health visitors we could bring about a major improvement in the long-term well-being of communities, because it is in the very early years that children are in most need of the love, care and attention that is essential if they are to thrive. Many health authorities are standing still, or even running down, the health visitor service and I sense here a lack of recognition that the Health Services have social as well as medical responsibilities.

Environmentalism means that you really care, not just for the environment, but for people as well. Caring for children and young people should mean that we do everything we can to keep children who are violent or uncontrollable, or have challenging behaviour, out of prison – and that if they do get custodial sentences that we do everything we can to make it less likely that they will re-offend on release.

Tackling social problems in a holistic way is one kind of future I would like to invent.

* * *

For years I dreamed of becoming an elected politician, so that I could bring Green thinking and Green policies to the consciousness of a wider public. In 1999, finally, my dream came true.

So what did I believe, that day in May 1999, that I could achieve?

Realistically, just that – a raising of awareness. In the event, media and public interest in me and my Green views was out of all proportion to the number of public votes I represented. During my first four-year term, and subsequently, I was given an astonishing platform to comment on just about everything from reusable nappies to genetically modified salmon. I found that there was massive interest in what we had to say – perhaps from a public jaded by years of ya-boo politics and stimulated by the advent of our new Scottish Parliament, perhaps because environmental issues were quite becoming ever more pressing.

I took every opportunity to be involved in every issue that was presented to me and in every aspect of Scottish life. One day I will maybe leaf through my 'Good News' files and again be humbled by the many thousands of thank you letters and emails – most beginning Dear Mr Harper! – I have received over the years. Many hundreds of individuals and organisations asked me to help and support their cause and these letters make it clear that my backing gave them encouragement and hope. It certainly often gave them publicity for their cause. For me, an important bonus of all the hard work has led to a wider recognition that Green politics have answers that are just as good – and sometimes better – than mainstream thinking offered by other parties.

I have tried to live by my principles. I have seized the opportunity to involve myself in a vast range of issues that deeply interest me personally and that lie beyond immediate environmental causes – architecture, engineering, music, theatre, education and, in particular, outdoor education. I have also been hugely privileged to have been given the opportunity to continue my life's mission as both a teacher and politician – enthusing and exciting younger generations. I have made countless school visits, often accompanied by my toy Emperor penguin as a prop to stimulate conversations about the plight of the environment. These visits have been a constant joy and I hope they will continue when I am no longer a paid politician.

I am committed at every step to demonstrating the idea of thinking globally and acting locally. Greens have a deeply considered world view that begins and ends in local communities – and, therefore, they have a legitimate and ever-strengthening role in politics and in government.

If I have laid down a small foundation that my colleagues can use as a stepping stone into a Green future, I will feel that my work has been worthwhile.

In my first eighteen months, on top of my parliamentary work, I made 132 visits to schools, colleges and universities, environmental groups and community groups of one kind or another. I held 33 meetings with small business groups and architectural and arts organizations, and delivered 70 keynote speeches.

Little changed in my final 18 months in Parliament – except that most of the meetings were in Parliament and I travelled the country less. In the early years I sat through most of the debates and every question time, making interventions wherever I could. In the third Parliament, I spent less time in the debating chamber and more catching up on the ever-increasing number of emails. In 1999 I got worried if the backlog exceeded 50 or 60 emails at the end of the week. Latterly I regarded a backlog of 400 with resigned equanimity.

One of the most common questions I have been asked is, 'What do you think your legacy is?' I hope this will become clearer with time. With my Green colleagues, I have assisted – and I hope, succeeded – with two things. First, in embedding the Scottish Green Party in the fabric of Scottish politics, and second in raising the profile of sustainability and our precious environment in the thoughts and minds of the people of Scotland and in raising those issues to a new level of understanding and empathy across the political spectrum

As Greens, we have had no 'big wins' – more a series of smaller ones that add up to a real achievement. Through debate and some successful amendments I have helped to make improvements to all sorts of legislation, such as the Water Environment Bill, the National Parks Bill and the Climate Change Bill and to influence government policy on things like the Organic Action Plan 2003, Ship to Ship Oil

Transfers 2007–8 and, with Patrick Harvie, to secure the creation of the Climate Challenge Fund of so far £27.4 million. The Climate Challenge Fund will continue to be renewed and is certainly one of our finest achievements. More than 600 community groups have now received money for mini-renewable energy schemes, community recycling projects, community amenity projects, allotments, orchards and local food projects the length and breadth of Scotland. This small investment has produced added value beyond even our own expectations and beyond crude measures of economic success.

In the course of my 12-year Parliamentary sojourn I managed to win a few votes on motions I lodged, but there were two I particularly remember. The first vote I won was to get Parliament to agree to look at Land Value taxation. It happened the day after my dear father died in January 2002. I had left his bedside in Sussex to return to Edinburgh to debate yearly Green Party business and was on my way back to England within an hour of speaking. The second happened in the course of my last Green Party business debate in January 2011, when I won a motion calling on Parliament to give consideration to the setting up of a grameen-style community development bank – based on the pioneering micro-financing organization of Bangladeshi Fulbright scholar Professor Muhammad Yanus – to assist young people aged 18–20 to set up their own business and encourage a strong diverse and localized economy in Scotland.

I am proud to have started these conversations and raise many other issues which I hope will continue to be debated in and out of our new Parliament for many years to come

There is a lot more to do.

Index

Index

205

207

Index